MW00622235

THE CONTINENTAL LEAGUE

The Continental League

A PERSONAL HISTORY ★ RUSSELL D. BUHITE

University of Nebraska Press   Lincoln & London

© 2014 by Russell D. Buhite

All rights reserved
Manufactured in the United States of America

∞

Library of Congress Cataloging-in-Publication Data
Buhite, Russell D.
The Continental League: a personal history /
Russell D. Buhite.
pages   cm.
Includes bibliographical references.
ISBN 978-0-8032-7190-6 (hardback: alk paper)—
ISBN 978-0-8032-7381-8 (pdf)—
ISBN 978-0-8032-7382-5 (epub) (print)—
ISBN 978-0-8032-7383-2 (mobi)
1. Continental League (Baseball league)—History.
2. Rickey, Branch, 1881–1965. I. Continental
League (Baseball league) II. Title.
GV875.C84B84 2014
796.357'640973—dc23
2013043806

Set in Sabon by L. Auten.

For Mary, who if the beatitudes have contemporary meaning will surely inherit the earth.

CONTENTS

Acknowledgments   ix

Prologue   1

1. An Odyssey through Life and Baseball   9

2. The Continental League Conceived
and Organized   34

3. The Horsehide Cartel Challenged   68

4. The Western Carolina League   106

5. The Continental League Undercut   145

Appendix   171

Notes   193

Bibliography   203

ACKNOWLEDGMENTS

I owe debts of gratitude to a number of individuals who have assisted in the completion of this book. Laura Welsh, a talented undergraduate history major at Missouri S&T, helped put my manuscript into final form. Professor James Giglio of Missouri State University read the manuscript with a critical eye and offered insightful comments on ways I might improve it. My friend and former teammate, George Ferrell, of Jamestown, North Carolina, an intelligent and thoughtful man and a fine ballplayer in his day, shared his memories of events in which we both participated and gave the manuscript his careful attention. His imprimatur on my efforts is, in many ways, more important to me than any other. My friend Beth Greene Wheeler of Forest City, North Carolina, daughter of Bruce Greene, the owner of the Forest City ball club in 1960, provided the photograph of her father and took the picture of the ballpark as it appears today. The photograph of the ballpark at Gastonia came to me as a result of a chance meeting with two young groundskeepers who were also quite good with the camera: Matthew Grant and Gary Humphries. Patricia Kelly of the National Baseball Hall of Fame located pictures of the key figures involved in the Continental League story.

Pat Bozeman of the University of Houston Libraries graciously assisted in my use of the George Kirksey Papers as well as securing the photographs of Kirksey and Craig Cullinan. Stephanie Walsh of the Kings Mountain Historical Museum provided pictures of John Moss. Matthew Brown of the Howard Baker Center at the University of Tennessee gave generously of his time to help in the use of the Kefauver Papers. Special thanks go to the *North Carolina Historical Review* with Anne Miller as its skillful and considerate editor, for publishing, in 2004, some of the material expanded upon in this study.

It would be remiss of me not to call attention to Clair Willcox, reinstated editor-in-chief of the University of Missouri Press, for his encouragement of my research and writing. He gave my manuscript his careful assessments in the early period of its maturation. I also wish to thank Rob Taylor, superb senior editor at the University of Nebraska Press, and his colleagues for making it into a book.

Finally, my most important acknowledgment goes to my wife, Mary London Buhite, who in 1960 won countless friends in Forest City as a Continental Leaguer's young spouse. She has provided comfort, companionship, love, friendship, not to say steady assurance, helping make life most pleasant not only during my final year in professional baseball but for over fifty years thereafter.

THE CONTINENTAL LEAGUE

Prologue

Events of 1959 and 1960, though memorable, do not lead to easy characterization of the era. In 1959 Alaska and Hawaii, in that order, became the forty-ninth and fiftieth states of the Union. Governor Earl Long of Louisiana was diagnosed with a psychiatric illness and committed to the state mental hospital. He promptly fired the hospital director and replaced him with a political crony, who quickly declared him perfectly sane and released him. Elizabeth Taylor took her fourth husband, stealing Eddie Fisher away from Debbie Reynolds. That was no contest. Buddy Holly released his last record, "It Doesn't Matter," and Bob Dylan graduated from high school in Hibbing, Minnesota. Fidel Castro came to power in Cuba after overthrowing the government of Fulgencio Batista. Then in the spring he made a goodwill tour of the United States, before eventually turning to the Soviet Union for primary sustenance. In September Nikita Khrushchev made a thirteen-day trip to the United States, where he visited a hog farm in Iowa and tried, without success, to enter Disneyland.

In 1960 the Playboy Club opened in Chicago, but domestically presidential politics dominated the year. Senator John F. Kennedy received the Democratic nomination for the presidency. He and Vice President Richard Nixon, the Republican nominee, held the first televised general election debates, an election that Kennedy won by a thread. On May 1 the Soviets shot down Francis Gary Powers, who was flying over Sverdlovsk in a U.S. U-2 spy plane, thus initiating a major Soviet-American incident embarrassing to the administration of President Dwight D. Eisenhower. Eisenhower approved a CIA-sponsored Cuban exile army that would train for an invasion of Cuba, and he placed an embargo on the importation of Cuban sugar. Because of mutual hostility, Cuban-American relations went into serious decline. Arnold Palmer won golf's Masters Tournament at Augusta; the Boston Celtics won the NBA title; and Floyd Patterson defeated Ingmar Johansson to regain the heavyweight boxing crown. In the world of baseball, the biggest story of 1959 and 1960 was the organization of a third Major League.

Known as the Continental League, this new organization is significant and worthy of attention because it would have provided an alternative economic model for the nation's greatest sport. It would have brought the beginning of a collective enterprise into professional baseball, the first such endeavor since the Players' League of the late nineteenth century. As president of the new league, Branch Rickey, paradoxically, given his conservative political views, introduced an innovative, quasi-radical new system. What he had in mind, and what the owners of Continental League franchises agreed to do, was the following: to secure a television contract in which all or nearly all the revenue was shared equally among the eight new ball clubs; and to impose a system in which a high percentage of all gate receipts, home and away, would be pooled and divided up equally, a logical move since the visiting team provided a major part of the entertainment value. This scheme was also a way to obviate domination by the big-market teams, to prevent the seeming control over markets exerted year after year by a club like the New York Yankees.

Beyond that, central direction of the operation for the common good would be evident in many other ways. A handful of scouts would identify amateur prospects, either through observation of the players' games or in tryout camps. These players would be put in a pool and then drafted and signed by the Continental League clubs according to their needs. All Minor League clubs and players would remain under the control of the Continental League, with the big league itself providing the funding for the Minor League operations, and the big league scouts assessing the talents and progress of all the players. Each step in a player's movement toward the big league would remain under the purview of the central organization. The central organization would keep extensive records on each player for his assignment. Ticket prices for all Minor League teams would derive from decisions in the central office, as would player salaries. All managers at the Major and Minor League levels would come under the control of the Continental League itself. Four Major League clubs would train together in Texas and four together in Florida, switching sites each following year. All business and player decisions during spring training would occur in consultation with Rickey.

Rickey and his colleagues were widely criticized for their initiation of this new model, which many called socialized baseball. There is great irony in all of this considering Rickey's background and his political and economic philosophies. Rickey's strength was not political economy; nor was it philosophy; nor was it history; nor was it law, even though he was trained as a lawyer. His strength lay in evaluating baseball talent and in enhancing his personal business interests. Consistency was not required of him. But his long-time political affiliation and his ardent speechifying create irony aplenty. A lifelong Republican, as a young man Rickey supported Theodore Roosevelt's muscular politics and voted for the former president in both of his presidential races, including in 1912. How much of Roosevelt's New Nationalism he understood then or even later is unclear.

In the 1920s Rickey found another political hero in Herbert Hoover. He liked Hoover's life story, the Horatio Alger quality of it, the small-town, rural roots of it. He was especially fond of Hoover's substantially laissez-faire economic philosophy and his belief that government should exert the role of an umpire and not of a player in the economy. Here he certainly showed a departure from Theodore Roosevelt's thinking. He absolved Hoover and the Republicans of blame for the economic catastrophe that befell the nation after 1929, and he came to deplore Franklin D. Roosevelt's New Deal. He hated the bureaucracy of the latter, the taxing programs, the central planning, the welfare state, especially the welfare state. He saw no need for Social Security, or the Wagner Act as special assistance to labor, or the minimum wage law, or any other parts of Roosevelt's domestic programs. On the other hand, he hated dictatorship and saw the need to stand up to Hitler, Mussolini, and the Japanese militarists, as FDR had begun doing by 1939 and 1940.

After World War II he became a vigorous cold warrior, in part because he saw the Soviet Union and the People's Republic of China as strategic national threats to U.S. interests, but also because he deplored communist ideology with its rejection of religion, human freedom, and the sanctity of the individual. Central to his beliefs, repeated often and with great gusto, was a rejection of the socialist economies of America's adversaries. He supported President Eisenhower and became a strong advocate for Richard Nixon in the presidential election of 1960. Had he lived to see a Nixon presidency, he would have become a skeptic of détente but might well have endorsed Nixon's balance of power strategy toward China and the Soviet Union.

Did Rickey consciously or subconsciously believe in many socialist tenets all along, as his most agitated establishment baseball critics alleged in 1960, and to what version of socialism might he have subscribed? There are many varieties of socialism, one of the most prominent being government or state ownership of the means of production. Another is cooperative enterprise with several entities sharing in decision making and in the benefits of production. Still another is public ownership of a given enterprise or enterprises. All are designed to modify the effects, often the harshness, of the totally free market.

What Rickey wanted in 1959–60 was the organization, the sharing of revenues, the control of labor and management that existed in large corporations. Though there may have been similarities between the two models, it was corporatism rather than socialism that he hoped to pursue in the Continental League. He saw the eight ball clubs in the new league as separate departments in a large corporation. Among them there would be no competing for players, no scrambling for advantage over gate receipts, no quarrelling over television revenue, no economic competition over anything. The only competition he envisioned in the Continental League would occur on the field of play.

Rational as the new system seemed and for all of the good it might have instituted, it could not, in all likelihood, have sustained itself for long. Like many such models it contained the seeds of its own undoing. Nor with all his talents, all his rhetorical skills, all his management experience, could Rickey have remained a viable leader of the new league. For one thing he would not have endorsed a dramatic new plan that included generous concessions to players; fairness to players would not have conformed to his corporatist views.

In any event, assuming it operated independent of Organized Baseball, which was the only realistic avenue available to it in 1959–60, and assuming someone other than Rickey attained leadership, the Continental League could have brought significant benefit and reform to baseball in a number of ways. In addition to providing over three hundred Major League jobs and probably as many in the Minor Leagues, the third league would have helped players and fans alike. Had it made a commitment to abide by the terms of the Sherman and Clayton anti-trust acts and had it limited the reserve clause to a one-year contract, the Continental League would have ameliorated the grievances of players without the traumatic clashes of the 1970s, 1980s, and 1990s; and it could have kept salaries within reason. Annual free agency for all players, or in any case for almost all players except for those few superstars with mutually agreed-upon long-term contracts, would have allowed the market to determine salaries. When all or nearly all players become free agents, they become, it is useful to remember, unemployed. If there were many multiples of shortstops, or pitchers, or catchers on the market each year, owners of ball clubs would have had no incentive to bid up prices or salaries. Salaries would have risen in the short run and perhaps in the long run, but compared to what happened at the end of the twentieth century and into the early twenty-first century they would have remained modest. The result would have been lower costs for fans, decent profit for owners, and more funds for player development.

What follows is the story of the Continental League. The book is part memoir, particularly in the initial chapter and in the section on the Western Carolina League (WCL), but sometimes directly, sometimes indirectly in the other chapters as well.

1

An Odyssey through Life and Baseball

In 1961 and 1962 Major League Baseball established four new franchises. In subsequent years it established ten more. Given the exponential growth in the American population over the last fifty years of the twentieth century, such expansion would seem inevitable. As a general rule, however, historians do not enthusiastically embrace inevitability, preferring instead to seek out cause and effect, agents of change, and the context of important decisions. Major League expansion, in its initial phase, did not just happen; it occurred because a group of wealthy and determined men and women in American and Canadian cities, led by a creative, articulate baseball legend, built an incipient rival organization that threatened the interests of the contemporary baseball establishment. The story of the Continental League has been told in bits and pieces, the best accounts those of journalist and scholar Michael Shapiro and independent historian Lee Lowenfish. Despite their excellent work, however, the story is in many ways incomplete.[1]

I was one of the original Continental Leaguers, and as both a participant and a historian, I believe I am better positioned than most to explain the life—and death—of this agent of change. Because I had been a professional Minor

League player in the three years prior to the beginning of the new league and because I signed with one of the Continental League franchises, my own odyssey through life and baseball was intertwined with Major League Baseball's expansion in 1961 and 1962.

I became interested in baseball while most boys are still studying dinosaurs. As a child of six or seven, my parents regularly took me to Sunday afternoon sandlot or semiprofessional games in the village of Wishaw, home of my mother's parents, located about three miles from our west central Pennsylvania farm. Wishaw had once been a thriving, though exceedingly ugly, little mining town of three hundred to five hundred or so people, containing rows of company houses, backyard privies, dirt streets, a small general store or two, a tavern, and a sizable ethnic population comprised of Italians, Poles, Hungarians, and Slovaks. From the time of my memory its population had become smaller, no more than two hundred residents. (It had been severely ravaged by the flu epidemic of 1918–20.) But it had a baseball team and had fielded a team for as long as any of the locals could recall. (The "semipros" among the players were those who had comparatively easy jobs in the mines and were employed for their baseball abilities.) The immigrants' sons refused to play soccer, a game they knew well; they loved the American game of baseball. I watched the games, usually with my parents, from a grove of trees, enjoying the shade and often a bottle of soda pop while witnessing the performance of the Wishaw nine. Most of the games were against other mining-town teams in a league whose name I cannot recall. Fans would often number a hundred but frequently no more than fifty. The team bought its baseballs with funds raised by passing the hat. All the players wore uniforms, with some of them unmatched. My favorite player on that team was the shortstop, Lester Finelli, a solid performer, a left-handed hitter, whose father owned one of the general stores.

At the impressionable age of nine or ten, I once witnessed a game in Wishaw that resulted in a serious interteam rhubarb and difficulty with an umpire. These games were always played with no more than two umpires, usually volunteers from the crowd of spectators who knew something of the rules. If the teams could secure only one umpire, he would station himself behind the pitcher's mound so as to call balls and strikes as well as plays at the bases. On the occasion of my recollection the umpire made a flawed ruling on an appeal play following a sacrifice fly. Tempers flared, the game eventually terminated at its midpoint, and a group of angry local fans put the umpire in serious jeopardy. They literally chased him up the road out of town, right on his heels as he sprinted away to save life and limb.

At age eight at the local one-room school located in Panic, about a mile in the other direction from our farm, I began playing a game resembling baseball. Our teacher, Ray Cramer, who taught all eight grades and could do pretty much as he wished in the school as long as he kept order, loved baseball. Hence, at lunchtime and recesses when the weather permitted, we always had a game. Sometimes lunch would go on until 1:30 or 2:00, and school lessons took secondary position. He was an excellent teacher, especially of history, but he liked baseball better than history or spelling or anything else. The game we played on that playground utilized a sponge-rubber ball, which under the rules could be thrown at a base runner and if the runner was struck by the ball he or she would be out. Otherwise the rules were largely the same as in other baseball games. I did not excel in these lunchtime contests because everyone—that is, the older boys—tried to make me, a natural left-hander, throw and hit right handed!

When I advanced to the fifth grade, all students in Panic's one-room school moved to a larger facility with a room for each grade in Anita, a mining community of three hundred to four hundred people about four miles away. The Panic school, which had functioned for nearly a century, was no longer sustainable. In Anita I began playing baseball almost every day. We played at recess and at noon starting in February or early March and running into June. We also played in September and early October. These were pickup games with no adult supervision, and I thrived in them. I learned a great deal by trial and error and without pressure. After a short time I was usually the first player picked in these school-yard games. We had a split-rail fence running across the outfield that served as a home run barrier. In the right-field corner the barrier was the girls' outhouse. (The school had indoor water fountains but no modern restrooms.) The better hitters, including my good friend George Roseman, would hit forty-five to fifty home runs in a "season." I rattled lots of balls around inside the girls' toilet, to our everlasting pleasure and the girls' shrieks of feigned outrage.

From age nine to eleven these school games provided my baseball experience. I delighted in them, developed social skills from them, made many lasting friends in the organizing and playing of them. When I was ten, my parents bought me my first glove, an Augie Galan model outfielder's glove. (Galan was an outfielder and infielder with the Chicago Cubs, the Brooklyn Dodgers, and the Cincinnati Reds in the 1930s and 1940s.) It was a primitive piece of equipment that had no lacing between the fingers and felt padding inside that would pull out when I extricated my sweaty hand. But I loved it; it was the first glove I had ever seen designed to fit on the right hand for a left-handed thrower. It came, as did many of my parents' purchases, from the Sears, Roebuck and Company catalog.

I remember the constant struggle in these school games to find and keep a playable baseball. We thrilled at the chance to play with a ball with a legitimate cover. When we knocked off the cover, one of us would sew it back on with fishing line. When the cover became totally unusable, we put rubber tape on the ball. When balls became waterlogged, as they often did, we baked them dry in our mothers' ovens.

Baseball, the playing of the game, acquiring adequate equipment, and the honing of my skills became the epicenter of my existence between ages nine and twelve. One of my uncles, Mervin Foltz, the husband of one of my father's sisters, who had played a bit and loved the game, encouraged me on a regular basis. He taught me many of the finer aspects of the sport and related his knowledge of its history and lore. This uncle took me to my first Major League Baseball games. On August 29, 1948, he and two of his longtime friends asked me to go with them to a doubleheader at Forbes Field in Pittsburgh to see the Pirates play the Boston Braves, the eventual National League pennant winner that year. The Pirates, who enjoyed a winning season in 1948 and finished in fourth place only eight and a half games behind the first-place Braves, played inspired baseball. They won both games—rookie right-hander Bob Chesnes, a 6–1 winner over Warren Spahn, in the first one, and journeyman lefty Vic Lombardi the winner by a 5–2 margin over Bill Voiselle in the second. I was already enthralled by baseball, my excitement for it unbounded, and that Sunday afternoon sealed my commitment to the game.

When my uncle Mervin was not present, my father played catch with me, and he taught me, at age eleven, to throw a pretty good curve ball. My father, a farmer, was always awfully busy, had never played baseball, but he had excellent athletic talent and was a good teacher when it came to throwing and catching. His own sports were hunting and fishing, which he indulged with great enthusiasm.

The summer of my twelfth year afforded me the chance of a lifetime. Little League baseball had been organized in our local towns, and Reynoldsville, a community of around three thousand people, located about five miles away, developed a league. To a young boy seldom off the farm, Reynoldsville resembled a metropolis; it was my parents' shopping area, the locale of their high school, whence they had graduated in 1935, and their social center. If they went to town, it was to Reynoldsville. One afternoon, after the league had started play, my uncle Mervin stopped by and asked if I wanted to go with him to join one of the teams, the Dodgers, at their practice. He had arranged it with the coach. I jumped at the opportunity. No one on that team was better than I. No one in the league was better. No one could run as fast. No one could throw or catch as well. No one could hit any better; indeed, I never struck out, not once, the whole summer. I played the season, led the league in hitting, made the All-Star team, and had a wonderful time. That spring I had gotten my first first-baseman's mitt. I played first and pitched. It disappointed but did not crush me when we lost in the regional playoffs to an All-Star team from Punxsutawney that went on to win the state championship—a team comprised of players who would later become my teammates.

Little League did two things for me: it helped further develop my baseball skills, and it reinforced my dissatisfaction with life on the farm. For as far back as I could remember, I disliked the farm. Now I despised it, a sentiment I never lost for the remainder of my life. As with a great many American boys of that era, life on the farm taught me one very important lesson: do whatever necessary to get away from it—to put the drudgery, the boredom, the isolation, the deprivation of social and intellectual skills it imposed, behind me. For a number of years—too many as it turned out—I saw baseball as my way out.

My distaste for the farm had nothing to do with my parents. They were wonderful, loving parents. They were devoted to each other. They never fought, and they provided a secure home for my two sisters, a younger brother, with encephalitis-induced mental retardation, and me. I was the oldest. One of my sisters was three years younger and the other eight years younger. My brother was thirteen years my junior. Both my parents were extremely bright, able, honest, hardworking people. My mother had established an excellent record through high school. My father, though he graduated with ease, never devoted himself to school, but his intellect was more wide-ranging, his interests more varied, his skills more diverse, than my mother's. He possessed a sophisticated sense of humor and a wonderful ability to tell a story. My mother, a red-haired young woman of nineteen when she married my father, was high-strung, emotional, sharp tongued, and could become quite abrasive. She epitomized the type A personality. But she was also a loving and caring person, and she indulged me, as mothers often do, when she should not have done so. As a mark of my parents' relationship, I can remember when I was sixteen and playing American Legion baseball seeing them walk from the parking lot to the bleachers, hand in hand. No other married couple of my acquaintance would have done that. I recall feeling some embarrassment, foolishly, at the sight.

Life had not been easy for my parents. My mother came from a family of eight children, seven girls and one boy. Born in 1918, she was the third oldest child of a hardworking, protective mother and a drunken, marginally effective father, whom she held in utter contempt. My knowledge of my maternal grandfather extended over thirty years. I do not recall ever seeing him sober. Though he seldom missed a day of work in the coal mines, not an easy work assignment and not an easy task given his drinking habit, he spent every evening and most of his weekends in the local tavern. He drank assiduously, spending a high percentage of his income on alcohol and thus depriving his family of many of life's necessities. In reaction my mother seldom permitted alcohol in our house, which was not a serious problem for my father, who was only an occasional drinker. She never spoke favorably of her father in my presence. She probably never knew serious hunger because the family always had some acreage for an extensive garden in that mining town, but she never had any luxuries, fancy clothes, or entertainment—or a chance to go to college.

My father grew up on our same family farm. Like many such farms in Pennsylvania, it produced a little of this and a little of that, sometimes a lot of each. Also born in 1918, he was the third child in a family of seven, the three oldest being boys. His life was one of struggle, through a farm price depression in the 1920s and a full-fledged economic crisis in the 1930s. He went to work in a coal mine directly out of high school at fifteen dollars per week, all of which he turned over to his parents. He worked on the farm during his off-hours. After marrying my mother in February 1938, he continued this pattern but in the early 1940s moved to a small town near Cleveland, Ohio (Chardon), and worked in defense plants in Cleveland. A medical condition made him 4-F, so he did not participate in the military in World War II. Despite the war and its rationing, there was always plenty of everything, it seemed, while we lived in Ohio. I recall bounteous tables as a young boy, and we had a good car—a 1941 Ford that my father bought new for nine hundred dollars. But my father never made or had much of what he called "cash money." He returned to Pennsylvania to take over the farm in 1945, as my grandparents recognized his multiple talents as more suited to that role than those of his siblings. The farm became his de facto, if not de jure, in 1952 with my grandfather's death. I say de facto because he never had a written contract conveying it to him; my grandmother technically held control until her death in 1970. My father made the farm prosperous and one of the best in the county as a dairy operation. My life on the farm began effectively in 1945, and it was not long thereafter that I received regular, rigorous work assignments. By age nine I drove a tractor and a pickup truck, helped with most of the barn chores, and did my share of work. I milked cows until I hoped I would never see another cow. I never considered myself good at farming activities and realized, certainly by age ten, that not only did I not want to become a farmer, but also that I would possess few of the skills necessary to succeed as one.

In fact, I had no idea as a boy what my true talents were. I knew I could play baseball, could play it very well indeed, and could do passably well at other sports to which I had been introduced. I excelled in school, enough to skip third grade in the one-room school and to earn As when I worked hard. Still, my report cards often cited deportment deficiencies, and one for seventh grade contained the ominous message to my parents: "bothers others" and "wastes time!" I recall in ninth grade my good friend and baseball teammate Jim Bowser telling me that when he grew up he wanted to become an engineer. I thought to myself, "What the hell is an engineer?" I knew he had no aspirations for a railroad career! I knew of no other engineers.

My high school life transpired in Punxsutawney, then a town of roughly ten thousand people located about seven miles south of our farm, known since the 1880s as the home of the weather-prognosticating groundhog. Though I often made the honor roll, I devoted far more time to baseball than I did to studying in my Punxsutawney years. In 1987, back in town to present the high school commencement address, I was amused when the young lady who introduced me produced my statement of career goals submitted thirty-two years earlier. It said, "Don't know!" Well, I did know back in 1955 that I wanted to continue playing baseball. I did not know if I would have the chance.

Baseball in Punxsutawney was for me and my teammates successful and exciting. After Little League I joined a teenage league sponsored by the Veterans of Foreign Wars. Among my teammates was a group of players who had won the Little League state championship and played in the 1950 Little League World Series in Williamsport, Pennsylvania, to help establish perennially winning teams. We went to the state finals two years running—in 1952 and 1953—at Harrisburg and Huntingdon respectively. We had an excellent chance at the state championship in 1953 when I hit a ball into left-center field that cleared an embankment and sailed into the Juniata River only to be quickly retrieved by a swimmer who threw the ball back onto the field of play. When the umpire ruled the hit a ground-rule triple instead of a home run (who ever heard of a ground-rule triple except when a fielder throws a glove at a ball?), all hell broke loose. The play kept us from scoring the tying run and contributed to our elimination and much protest both on the field and back home—all to no avail.

From 1953 until 1956 I sometimes played on two teams each year. American Legion baseball began in Punxsutawney in 1953, and I started playing regularly on that team while also holding down a position in the teenage league. In 1954 I played on a county league team sponsored by a local shoe store owner while also playing Legion ball. In 1955 and 1956 I played exclusively for the Legion team as we played not only in the regular Legion circuit but also in the local amateur organization called the Jefferson County League. We had excellent players on all these teams: a middle infield comprised of my friends Jim Bowser at shortstop and Jim Costanzo at second, an outstanding double play combination; a first-rate catcher named Jack Meenan; a speedy third baseman named Eddie Curry; a superb outfielder and hitter, Vinnie Villella, and a strong pitcher named Tony Bodenhorn. I remember a Legion game against a team from Reynoldsville in which our two, three, four, and five hitters (I regularly hit third) each had four hits, the only time I ever saw that accomplished in all the years I played. I also remember a no-hitter by Tony Bodenhorn, the only one I ever played in, including during my days in Organized Baseball. Our teams were not always well coached, as I soon learned once in professional baseball, but we made up for these shortcomings with ability and desire.

Our best team was the one assembled in 1955, the year of my high school graduation, and it was also one of my personal best amateur seasons. Against older, more experienced competition we did exceedingly well in the Jefferson County League. Several of our players were among the league leaders in all categories. I hit .408 in the first half of a split season, leading the league in at bats and hits. I finished the year with a .356 batting average with several doubles and triples and two home runs. We breezed through the Legion season and won (by a score of 12–1) the game that would have sent us to the state championship playoffs in Allentown. But our victory did not hold, thanks to a protest by our opponents. The opposing pitcher, probably not deliberately, hit our pitcher with a pitched ball. Our catcher and my good friend Jack Meenan sprinted from our dugout to, in his words, "kick the shit out of that kid." No fight ensued, as our coach intercepted him, but Legion rules apparently forbade such exhibitions of poor sportsmanship, and a regional rules committee forced a replay of the game. We lost 3–2. Meanwhile, in the protested game the opposing team's fans, of whom there were about three hundred, went berserk and threatened all of us with bodily harm. We left the field in DuBois, Pennsylvania, under police escort. Baseball was serious business in our part of the country.

During that year I was selected to participate in a special Legion All-Star Game organized for the benefit of Major League scouts. I played most of the game but did not have an opportunity to distinguish myself either in the field or at the plate. I had no idea if any scout was impressed. Several asked me mundane questions afterward, but that was all. The previous year I had attended a Philadelphia Phillies tryout camp run by Cy Perkins, a scout and ex–Major League catcher. I hit a triple and a single in the course of the game there, though I had not yet reached my sixteenth birthday. But Perkins was pleased and said he would be in touch. I later had a tryout with the Pittsburgh Pirates at Forbes Field. In the latter tryout I showed up well in timed running, in throwing, and in the fielding drill but got no good pitches to hit in the batting cage. I hit only a few balls hard and none for any distance. It was a special thrill for me to dress in the Pirates' clubhouse and to meet Hall of Famer Harold "Pie" Traynor, who said to me after the workout: "I'll be seeing you, kid, for sure." His words sustained me for quite a while. But the Pirates did not sign me in the summer of 1955. Nor did any other club tender an offer.

As the summer of 1955 passed, I decided to go to college. Standing in the kitchen talking to my mother, I said, "Classes are starting tomorrow at the Penn State campus in DuBois [about fifteen miles away]. Should I go to college?" Her response was typical of my parents' guidance on matters of education, career, or whatever I might do with my life. They had never encouraged or discouraged me at baseball. They had seen me play no more than five times. They had never attended a PTA meeting or said a word one way or another as I chose a college preparatory course in high school. All I remember of their advice was, while in elementary school, that if I ever got a spanking at school I would get another one when I got home. There was an admirable side—and beneficial one for me too—in this curiously laissez-faire approach. At any rate, my mother replied, "Well, you can go to college if you want to." That is how my academic experience began.

I turned seventeen less than two months before enrolling in college and knew almost nothing about the professions, academe, or the world at large. I had never handled money, never written a check, never been in an elevator—the list could go on and on. I liked chemistry in high school, so I decided to major in chemistry. I took two college chemistry courses and did very well in them. I took all the required general education courses and spent much of my time thinking about baseball. Had I had some advice, had I known what I came to know later, had I been interested in combining college and baseball, I would have gone to a top-quality college or university and played baseball. Instead, for reasons that I cannot recall, probably the minimal tuition, I transferred after that first year to Clarion State College, now Clarion University. My plan was to sign a professional baseball contract as soon as I could do so—to begin playing 120 to 140 games a year, to make money doing what I liked best in life.

I did not become interested in baseball because of the absence of a clock regulating its rhythms, or to defeat time, or for its ballet-like nature, or for any of the various and sundry qualities with which poetic license has invested it. Baseball appealed to me (and still does) because it made demands that I considered challenging: it required, I thought, the greatest number of physical and psychological attributes, in combination, of any sport; it was (and is) virtually impossible to master—and it was fun. Most importantly, for some reason I became pretty good at it. It gratified my ego, and it satisfied my need to escape from the farm.

The more I learned of baseball history, the statistics and the lore, the more I came to appreciate that contemporary players competed not just against one another but against the legends of the past—not only the professional legends but those on the local level as well. Every statistic of the game has been recorded, so performance is always measurable, at least to some degree. Baseball also taught me, more than anything else in life, about failure, as even my best performances usually meant failure two-thirds of the time and even my teams' successes usually meant successes no more than two-thirds of the time. But that was and is the extent of my romantic attachment to the game.

It is at the same time a wonderful game, requiring tremendous skill. It was and is my favorite sport. Its rules have remained basically intact for over a hundred years, and while the quality of play has changed over time, the game remains balanced; the size and speed of players have not altered the game as they have in basketball and football. But baseball is no more "perfect" than football, basketball, soccer—or quoits—and it no more comports with the national character or the best of what is American than stock car racing. Moreover, at the professional level it has been presided over by some of the most selfish, venal, self-serving, conceited, and shortsighted "leaders" of any athletic activity. Its practitioners, the professional players, are not individuals whose behavior has always proven admirable. Many have been egomaniacal, juvenile, and often morally corrupt, at least as selfish as their "leaders."

I spent much of my time in my youth thinking about baseball, but not all of it. I also devoted a great deal of thought to a girl I had met in high school, Mary Elizabeth London, who sat two seats away from me in physics class—a young lady with dark brown eyes, pitch-black hair, and the brightest, most luminescent smile I had ever seen. We liked each other instantly; we began dating while juniors in high school, continued our relationship in college (she went to a different college), and through thick and thin. She became my companion, helpmate, and best friend. We have been together for well over fifty years; she is the mother of our three children and has won the hearts of everyone who has ever had the privilege of knowing her. She lived one year of professional baseball with me—she too was one of the Continental Leaguers.

I have often noted in responses to queries about my baseball career that three Major League organizations saw fit to release me, but have taken solace in the knowledge, lo these many years, that three also saw fit to sign me.

In 1957 I signed with the New York Giants, former in-fielder and then Minor League manager Buddy Kerr doing the signing. He liked my hustle, my running speed, my defensive skill at first base, and the strength of my throwing arm, and he thought I would develop as a hitter. I played the 1957 season at Pensacola in the Alabama-Florida League; in Hastings, Nebraska, of the Nebraska State League, a rookie league; and in Muskogee, Oklahoma, of the Sooner State League. Because of a groin injury I played sparingly at Muskogee, and after I "recovered" the Giants released me.

The 1957 season provided a substantial learning and growth experience. It was my first time away from home. I encountered all types of people, developed friendships, learned of the cynicism and hard realities of Minor League Baseball, and began learning how to play the game at a much higher level than I had ever previously experienced. I played on the same teams with Robert "Bo" Belinsky, John-ny Weekly, Neil Wilson, and Verle Tiefenthaler, all of whom later made it to the Major Leagues. I played against Larry "Moose" Stubing, Steve Barber, Jim McKnight, Jim Kaat, Billy Williams, and Bobby Knoop, among others, who also made it to the big leagues, the last three of whom became stars. I played for one manager I considered a good guy and two I wasn't so fond of. Lou Fitzgerald at Pensacola fit the former category; Leo Schrall at Hastings and Andy Gilbert at Muskogee were in the latter. Schrall was the head base-ball coach at Bradley University who was earning summer money. His approach was to badger and scold. He once screamed at our talented center fielder, Mike Levins, when Levins misjudged a fly ball: "Any little leaguer could have caught that fucking ball." One of our outfielders threw a ball out of the ballpark on a play at the plate. It was funny, so egregious it was hilarious. Schrall berated the player for the rest of the game. He yelled obscenities at me one night after I lost a high bouncing ball in the lights: "If you can't see at night we can't use you. You might be the best fielding first baseman in the organization, but I'm going to play [Humberto] Sama. We have more money in him anyway."

Gilbert, who had played a few games for the Boston Red Sox in 1946 and been a player-manager in the Minor Leagues for years after that, spent a good deal of his time bragging about his exploits: "When I played for Muskogee in the Western Association in 1952 people everywhere said Mantle never hit them that far." (Mickey Mantle had played for Joplin in the Western Association in 1950.) I wondered why the established players on the team, when I arrived, avoided him. I soon found out. But Gilbert did offer me some valuable advice: "You may hit the ball 375 to 400 feet once a month. You are never going to be a power hitter. Concentrate on hitting line drives. Hit down on the ball."

I also learned some things about base running from Gilbert, who knew the game better than he knew people, but by far my best tutor during that 1957 season was my good friend and veteran Minor League player Bob Zuccarini, with whom I played at Pensacola. Zuccarini was not a great outfielder, could not run well, and did not have a strong throwing arm. But he could hit. He led the Alabama-Florida League in hitting with an average of .352 and ended the season with twenty-seven home runs and eighty-seven runs batted in. As a wide-eyed eighteen-year-old kid, I found him one of the easiest players to talk to and listen to of any teammate ever. He had been around. As often as possible I sat beside him on the team bus, and we talked baseball. He talked about never swinging at a breaking ball on the first pitch, what pitch to look for in certain situations, when to try to steal third base, to try to stretch doubles into triples only with one out, how to judge the outfielders' positioning and get a break off second base on an apparent base hit and so on and so on. Whether he knew it or not, he was an outstanding teacher and a strong influence on me. I was hitting .296 at Pensacola and playing well at first base prior to my assignment to Hastings.

Over that first season I learned the lexicon of professional baseball as well: "soft hands," "good hands," "quick feet," "good wheels" (for running speed), "a cannon" (strong throwing arm), "a gun" (strong throwing arm), "play deep and cut across" (for a slow-footed outfielder), "put some grass in your hat" (for an outfielder staggering under a fly ball), "roll him into left field" (break up a double play), "stick it in his ear" (for a knock down pitch), "punch and Judy" (for a light singles hitter), "rope" (for a line drive), "quail" (for a bloop hit), "cunny thumber" (for a soft throwing pitcher with poor stuff), "a jaker" (for someone who habitually took himself out of the lineup—took time off), "a unie" (for a uniform), "three circles and a dive" (for a catcher who had trouble with pop-ups), "charge the ball" (for a pitcher who had a line drive hit at him), "loading it up" (for a pitcher who put moisture on the ball), "hang in there," "what happens on the road stays on the road," "a hotel with room service," "hot dog" (for a show-off or player with a flair), "bush league" or simply "bush" (for unbecoming, unprofessional behavior).

Travel was one of the best experiences that first season. I learned to love the beach at Pensacola, Fort Walton Beach, and Panama City. I rode a series of Greyhound buses from Pensacola to Hastings, Nebraska, across country I had never seen before. In central Missouri on the way to Kansas City, somewhere along old Route 40, the bus driver stopped at a service/bus station/café facility for a twenty-minute rest stop. I came out of the café after a cup of coffee and piece of pie to see the bus disappear down the road in the distance, with all my bags and baseball gear on board. I was stuck in the middle of Missouri! The station operator did little to ease my mind when he said he thought another bus might be along in thirty minutes. I was lucky: another did come along, and we pulled into the station in the next city just as the first bus was leaving. When I jumped out and got aboard, the driver apologized for "losing" me: "I wondered what happened to you."

Travel from Hastings to Muskogee was equally eventful. I rode a fairly comfortable train, my first train ride ever, from Hastings to Kansas City. The one that took me from Kansas City to Muskogee, Oklahoma, however, appeared to be borrowed from some museum, outfitted as it was with wooden straight-back seats and no club or dining car. I arrived in Muskogee to 102-degree temperatures in midafternoon after riding all night and much of the day, uncomfortable in the extreme, and starving. I checked into the old Jefferson Hotel in downtown Muskogee, which had no air conditioning, caught a cab to the ballpark, still without eating, and met Gilbert. Not one to "coddle" a player, he greeted me with, "I assume you are ready to play." So I played that night.

Of all my experiences in this first of my years in Organized Baseball, none came close to matching the horrors of racial segregation in the American South. I had grown up in an all-white county. I had never attended elementary or secondary school with an African American. I had known only a few blacks in my college years. My experience with and my knowledge of segregation or of the importance of race in American society existed only at the abstract level. My ideas, such as they were, had come from my family, our church, and the old-line abolitionist tradition; they were absolute: a person's skin color had no bearing whatever on that person's character, ability, or anything else—certainly not on his or her access to civil society. I could hardly believe my eyes at the "white" and "colored" drinking fountains, and I could not contain my revulsion at the white-only cafés run by low-life proprietors who refused service to our black players. Then there were the sideline trips to the all-black section of town, where we put black players up in rooming houses. Nothing brought racism to my consciousness quite so directly, however, as an experience with a black teammate and friend with whom I swapped sport coats for an evening out. I learned from my southern teammates and others that this was "unacceptable" behavior—and dangerous! Why did black fans sit in the left-field bleachers, always the left-field bleachers, by themselves? No one could answer that one. Nor could anyone tell me why the "nigra" high schools were such ramshackle edifices.

From 1957 until 1960 I attended college only during the fall semester, dropping out at midyear to prepare for the next baseball season. In the winter of 1958 I worked extremely hard on physical conditioning. I ran and jumped rope daily in our barn, did push-ups and sit-ups, squeezed hand grips to strengthen my hands, wrists, and forearms. At that time lifting free weights was discouraged in baseball on the assumption that such activity limited flexibility. In any event, having signed in the off-season with the Baltimore Orioles, I went to spring training at Thomasville, Georgia, ready to have a good season. On my first day in camp, assigned to the Knoxville Smokies of the South Atlantic League, I had two hits in a game with one of the other Orioles Minor League clubs and played an excellent game at first base. George Staller, former Major League out-fielder and manager of the Knoxville club, congratulated me on my efforts. Eventually assigned to one of the lower-classification clubs, Pensacola, which had become over the winter a member of the Orioles organization, I went on to have a truly outstanding spring. I recall hitting two or three home runs and a couple of triples and never failing to hit in any of the spring training games. Earl Weaver, manager of the Dublin club in the Georgia-Florida League and lat-er the highly successful Orioles manager, gave me enthusi-astic reinforcement and told me at one point how pleased he would be to have me on his roster. That Orioles Minor League camp was filled with future Major Leaguers. Ev-eryone in the organization seemed to like my play and my hustling, all-out effort. It made no difference. At the very end of spring training, one member of the brass—I cannot recall which one—informed me that because the organiza-tion had invested bonus money in a large number of play-ers and there were so few ball clubs available on which to place me, it was "unfortunately" necessary to let me go. The news devastated me. I could play no better than I had just played. No one in the whole Minor League complex had done better. The bonus player who went on to play first base at Pensacola hit .226 for the 1958 season with one home run in 412 at bats.

Through the remainder of the 1958 season, I played am-ateur baseball back home in Pennsylvania, worked on the farm, saw Mary every evening, and contemplated my fu-ture. I was so discouraged with my baseball experience that I considered "retiring," giving it up. Had I not been only twenty years old and so enamored of the game, I proba-bly would have done so. Had I not possessed some residual confidence in my abilities, I certainly would have done so.

In 1959 I signed a contract with the Washington Senators and played at Sanford, Florida, in the Florida State League. I played reasonably well, hit .261, and was getting my game together when Washington made some changes, and before season's end I again received the pink slip. The Florida State League was and is a strong (now Class A) Minor League, and several future and former Major Leaguers were playing in the league in 1959: Vic Davalillo, Al Ferrara, Clarence "Cho Cho" Coleman, Bob Lipski, John Boozer, Joe Bonikowski, Lamar Jacobs, Horace Clarke, Von McDaniel, Tommy Helms, and Tom Hamilton among others. Although we had a number of very talented players at Sanford, including pitchers Bonikowski, Bob Pearson, my friend Jim Cundari, and Jacobs, an outfielder, we did not have a good ball club—and we developed the habit of losing, expecting to lose and just waiting for it to happen, even in games we led. We had too much fun off the field, did too much carousing, too much beer drinking, and gave up on the season too early. The Washington club did not help by sending in new players and releasing several of those already on the roster. I will never forget Sherry Robertson's appearance at a couple of our home games, wearing his dark sunglasses at night games and evaluating players. Robertson, adopted son of tightwad owner Calvin Griffith, held the position of farm director. I remember his lecture on how we needed to apply ourselves or, as he put it, "You will all be gone." During one of his visits (on June 24) Robertson brought in Lamar Jacobs, an outfielder from Ohio University whom Washington had signed for the then-princely sum of twenty-five thousand dollars in bonus money. In exchange Robertson took one of our outfielders with him, a fellow named Bob Keyes who had tremendous natural ability including a canon-like throwing arm, to pitch batting practice for the big club over the remainder of the season. The hope was to convert Keyes into a pitcher. As it turned out, Keyes never hit well enough to play the outfield and could not pitch well enough to make the Major Leagues as a pitcher.

By this time I had developed some knowledge of how baseball was supposed to be played, and though not cosmopolitan in any sense I was no longer the eighteen-year-old boy just off the farm. But I remember well a base-running lesson that season. We were playing the Cardinals' ball club, Daytona Beach. I was on first when our manager signaled for the hit and run. I ran on the pitch. The Daytona veteran second baseman and manager, Ray Wilson, ran to the second base bag and held his glove as if to accept a throw; I slid in to second, pretty as you please, only to be doubled up as the ball had been hit on a soft line drive to the right fielder. I knew, in theory, that one always had to pick up the ball off the bat on a hit and run play. I simply failed to do it. I never let myself be embarrassed that way again.

The low point of that season, apart from my eventual release, came after a tough loss one night in Palatka. We traveled in two Volkswagen buses, a player driving one of them, and several of us made certain we rode in the one without the manager. On the drive home we allowed the other bus to speed on ahead. We stopped and bought some beer—a lot of beer. Then we stopped at a roadside park and drank it. We arrived back in Sanford to unload our gear in the clubhouse at about 4:00 a.m., in sad shape indeed. On the blackboard was a note calling our attention to a 10:00 a.m. workout. We all made the workout, but we were a sorry-looking bunch that next morning; the heat and humidity, not to mention the alcohol, nearly killed us. My hotel in Sanford, still standing but dilapidated and leaning a little when I returned for a visit in the spring of 1990, was like the one in Muskogee, un-air-conditioned. (That hotel, The Montezuma, has since burned to the ground.)

After Washington released me—making it now releases from the Giants, the Orioles, and the Senators—I went home and with no job, still a year or so to go in college, no income and not much prospect of one, got married. I always saved enough baseball income to pay my tuition, but I certainly brought no sizable assets to a marriage. Mary had earned her degree in elementary education and gotten a job teaching first grade. So I went back to school at Clarion, this time with the intent of completing my course work by going the full year. I guessed I would become a teacher. I was an English and history major by now, subjects in which I had developed substantial interest, and thought I might eventually get a job in a high school. Maybe I would go on for a masters' degree and coach college baseball, a thought that came to the front of my mind when the Clarion baseball coach asked me to help him with the team during the spring of 1960. Then I received a call from the Forest City aka Rutherford County ball club of the newly revived Western Carolina League, which would be affiliated with Denver's team in the Continental League, asking me to play. Because Mary was supportive, because I knew I had improved as a player and did not yet want to quit, I leapt at the chance. I arranged to take all my finals—six of them—on one day, a week or so before the end of the semester, and then drove south to join the ball club on May 1.

By 1960 I had been released by three Major League organizations and had been scouted by several others that recognized my lack of home run power. Although my professional experience had been largely at the beginning level, I had played baseball with truly outstanding competition, had shared the field with exceptionally talented players. In retrospect perhaps it would have been better for me to combine baseball and college. But in those days the most talented players in the United States were not in college programs; they were in professional baseball at various levels; and most of them started in the lower-classification leagues. (I have seen hundreds of Minor League games over the years since I stopped playing, including several in the Florida State League. Pitchers now seem better at changing speeds, but otherwise I see little difference in the quality of play.) With a few exceptions, college baseball did not amount to much in the late 1950s and early 1960s. Seasons were short, usually no more than eighteen to twenty games, facilities were poor, and the coaching was mediocre at best. I knew in the spring of 1960 that making the Major Leagues, even one titled the "Continental League," was a remote possibility, but I was still young and wanted to play. Lightning might strike. I might still have a baseball career.

2

The Continental League Conceived
and Organized

Organized Baseball in 1959–60 was sick. It consisted, at
the top, of what Republican congressman Patrick Hillings
of California called "the horsehide cartel"—a collection
of sixteen teams located, with four exceptions, east of the
Mississippi River and held together by the practice of reserving players and maintaining territorial rights. Territorial rights meant that each Major League club could keep a
competitor out of its area. Reserving players meant signing
them to contracts that bound them for life to the team that
signed them. Some ball clubs, most particularly the New
York Yankees, were rich, thanks to the huge metropolitan
area in which they played, and they played in the World Series nearly every year. Some clubs were poorer, most particularly the Pittsburgh Pirates, the Washington Senators,
and the Kansas City Athletics.

Over the decade from 1949 to 1959, Major League attendance had declined by 20 percent. College football and
basketball grew ever more popular, and football, especially professional football, began for the first time to compete
for the entertainment dollar. Boating had become a popular
pastime, as had bowling, golf, and other participant sports.
Television kept people at home, and Organized Baseball,

despite televising a Saturday game of the week, had not yet begun to realize proper use of the new medium. Nor was it likely to make better use of the medium until television technology grew more sophisticated.

In 1960 the population of the United States had increased by over seventy-five million since the establishment of the American League in 1900–1901. Far more young men were playing baseball than ever before, despite the lure of football and basketball; far more hoped to play professionally than ever before. Yet in 1960 college baseball, as noted, amounted to little more than club-level activity. The professional Minor Leagues had declined in number from a high of fifty-nine leagues in 1949 to twenty-one in 1959 and twenty-one again in 1960. Attendance in Triple-A and Double-A leagues had dropped by over 50 percent. In lower-level leagues it was worse. Many B, C, and D leagues simply disappeared. Major League clubs had not begun to answer, indeed seemed incapable of answering, the question of where future players were to develop.

If baseball were to regain its standing as the national game, if it hoped to keep its grip on the youth of America, it had to make some dramatic changes. Baseball's salvation could and would, eventually, come from expansion to more American cities. But there was a right way to do expansion, and a wrong way. The right way was to follow the example set by Ban Johnson in establishing the American League.

Born in Norwalk, Ohio, in 1864, and raised in the Cincinnati area, Byron Bancroft "Ban" Johnson attended Marietta College in southeastern Ohio, where he played baseball, and then studied law at the University of Cincinnati. Though he never completed his law degree, the rigor of legal study helped prepare him for careers in journalism and baseball. During the 1890s he wrote for newspaper sports pages in Cincinnati, where he befriended Charles Comiskey, manager of the Cincinnati club of the National League. Comiskey and John Brush, owner of the Reds, assisted Johnson in becoming president of the Western League, a struggling but important Minor League, in 1894. Johnson, who had come to deplore the foul language and rowdy behavior in the National League, since 1876 baseball's one large, remaining organization, set out to make the Western League a model of decorum. He succeeded by banning the sale of alcohol at ballparks and fining players and managers for unbecoming behavior on the field.

In 1900, to give his organization greater prestige and to prepare for Major League status, Johnson renamed the Western League the "American League." He arranged to put franchises in Chicago, Cleveland, Boston, Philadelphia, and Baltimore, formerly the exclusive domain of the National League. This move was made possible in part because in 1900 the National League, which had encompassed twelve teams, contracted to eight. Johnson's new American League operated as a Minor League in 1900 but soon became Major. Outraged that the National League could draft players from the Minor Leagues for as little as five hundred dollars—a payment not to the player but to the Minor League club—Johnson, who had much grander plans anyway, decided to operate as a Major League in 1901. To do this, he and the owners in his circuit repudiated the National Agreement of 1892, which governed professional baseball.

As president the corpulent, autocratic Johnson ran a tight ship in his new league. He demanded and received loyalty and full authority from his owners and managers, among them Connie Mack, Clark Griffith, and Charles Comiskey. Johnson's key decision in 1901 was to operate under independent standing. This allowed him to move into National League territory and to sign as many National League players, despite their reputed reserve status, as he wished to sign—with the proviso that no contract would last more than five years. Thus the American League, an "outlaw organization," set about signing a great many National Leaguers, including the great star of the Philadelphia Phillies club Napoleon Lajoie, whom Johnson recruited for Connie Mack's Philadelphia Athletics.

In 1901 the American League consisted of successful ball clubs in Chicago, Boston, Detroit, Philadelphia, Baltimore, Washington, Cleveland, and Milwaukee. Ticket prices were set at twenty-five cents, and players and managers ostensibly kept their behavior clean—on and off the field. Despite an all-out effort by the National League to undercut his new league, both in the courts and through political deals, Johnson held on, and the American League outdrew the senior circuit at the gate in 1901. The quality of play was high, competition was keen, and more young men than ever before were given a chance to play professional baseball. In a move to solidify the organization's standing and prestige, Johnson arranged in 1903 to move the Baltimore club to New York, where the transplanted franchise became known as the New York Highlanders—until 1913, when the name became the New York Yankees. Among the players given a chance to play on the expansion New York Highlanders club, and one of Ban Johnson's greatest admirers, was Branch Rickey.

Unable to destroy the new league and beset by internal squabbling, the National League owners in 1903 decided to make peace. The result was a new National Agreement that, among other things, brought ratification of the reserve system and territorial rights for both leagues and recognized a Minor League structure that permitted continued classification within the Minors. It also instituted a new system for drafting Minor League players. This meant that National and American League teams could, for a set price, draft Minor League players, and Minor League clubs could draft from lower-classification clubs. The American League had thus, in three short years, received recognition and equal standing with the National League. A corollary to this arrangement was the beginning shortly thereafter of the World Series. Expansion proceeded in this way between 1900 and 1903.[1] It was done less rationally in 1960.

The impetus for expansion in 1959–60 derived from the move, beginning with the 1958 season, of the New York Giants to San Francisco and the Brooklyn Dodgers to Los Angeles, leaving New York a one-team town; and from the fertile brain of legendary baseball executive Branch Rickey, who had long believed that Major League Baseball could not remain viable unless it grew. Rickey's perceived mode of expansion, not coincidentally, mirrored that of Ban Johnson. The so-called lords of contemporary baseball had other ideas.

In August 1957, after years of marginal income and even more years playing in the antiquated Polo Grounds, Horace Stoneham announced that he was moving his Giants to San Francisco. They would play in the San Francisco Seals stadium of the Pacific Coast League until a new ballpark— Candlestick Park—was constructed. Stoneham, who had league approval for the move, had watched the highly successful transfer of the Braves from Boston to Milwaukee in 1953 and their multifold attendance increase. Blessed with newfound money, the Braves had put together a talented ball club that was on its way to winning the pennant in 1957— and again in 1958.

In 1957 Walter O'Malley also received National League approval to move his Dodgers out of Brooklyn. Indeed, the approval came with the caveat that the Dodgers could move to Los Angeles if the Giants went along to the West Coast, so the two ball clubs worked in unison to desert New York. "Desert" may be a too-strong term to describe what actually occurred since O'Malley had sought to build a new ballpark in Brooklyn, only to be stymied in his efforts by Robert Moses, the powerful parks commissioner who had in mind a fancy new stadium in Flushing Meadows in Queens. In any event, O'Malley received a lucrative deal from Los Angeles, which included land for a new stadium in Chavez Ravine, not far from downtown, and access to play in the Coliseum until the new ballpark was completed. O'Malley formally announced the move in early October 1957.

When the Giants and the Dodgers relocation became known, indeed well before the formal announcements were made, New York mayor Robert Wagner swung into action, hoping to get a replacement for at least one of the departing teams. He contacted the powerful Brooklyn banker and former New York City police commissioner George V. McLaughlin, a tall, imperious, sometimes dignified man of seventy years, often referred to as "George the Fifth," to help in this endeavor. McLaughlin in the 1930s had been head of the Brooklyn Trust Company, which held control of the then-woeful Dodgers. He hired Walter O'Malley, a young bankruptcy attorney, to help put the franchise on sounder financial footing. Little did he know what O'Malley would do with the beloved Dodgers once O'Malley became principal owner of the club in 1950.

McLaughlin was accustomed to having his way, which was of course why Wagner asked for his help. He tried to arrange a purchase of the Giants from Stoneham, only to be rebuffed. He tried working with Warren Giles, president of the National League, to identify a team willing to relocate to New York, again with no success. He then turned to Branch Rickey, whom he had known when Rickey ran the Dodgers.

After a losing battle with his hated rival O'Malley for control of the Dodgers—though the financial arrangements raise doubts about who outsmarted whom—Rickey in 1950 had signed on as general manager of the Pittsburgh Pirates. His old friend and fellow Ohioan John Galbreath was the Pirates' principal owner. Rickey achieved little success in Pittsburgh, or at best modest success, and Galbreath fired him in 1955. For the first time in his adult life, he was out of baseball. McLaughlin believed, however, that because the Pirates' attendance was so poor—in 1957 they had drawn only slightly more than eight hundred thousand fans, down one hundred thousand from 1956—and were hemorrhaging money, Rickey might help him convince Galbreath to move the franchise to New York. The New York Pirates could play in Brooklyn for a while and then go to Moses's new park in Flushing Meadows. Galbreath, as it turned out, was not interested in moving.[2]

Mayor Wagner then met with McLaughlin and formed a committee whose task was to take whatever steps necessary to bring a Major League team to New York. This committee consisted of some of New York's most powerful men: James Farley, President Franklin D. Roosevelt's campaign manager in 1932 and 1936, his postmaster general, and a longtime political force in New York; Bernard Gimbel, owner of Gimbel's Department Store; Clinton Blume, a former Major League pitcher and most recently a real estate developer. Blume, a five-feet-eleven, 175-pound athlete from Brooklyn, had attended Colgate University and then pitched for the Giants in 1922 and 1923. He achieved a 3-0 record with a 3.00 earned run average while appearing in one game for the 1922 National League pennant winners and in twelve games for the 1923 winners. The other committee member, the chair and dominant figure over the next several years, was William Shea.[3]

Shea was an ambitious, highly successful lawyer, a tall, handsome fellow of fifty when he took on this assignment. He had grown up in Manhattan, a good student and, though not a baseball player, a pretty good athlete. He played lacrosse, football, and basketball. He had attended New York University before transferring to Georgetown to earn his undergraduate degree and then study law. After college Shea returned to New York, where he held governmental law jobs before beginning his own firm in 1940. He was not a litigator or a scholar but a mediator, which is often a lawyer's most prized skill. He also possessed a winning personality, with a prepossessing broad grin and a genuinely friendly demeanor. Everyone liked Bill Shea, because without much effort, he was likable. Those qualities, however, did not mean that he could convince a National League owner to move to New York.

For a time the Cincinnati Reds seemed a live possibility to fill the void in New York. At the end of the 1957 season their owner, Powell Crosley Jr., reiterated his complaint about the Reds' ballpark, Crosley Field. Knowledge that Shea was actively seeking a National League team for New York, which became clear to all the owners at baseball's winter meetings in December 1957, led Crosley to hint that the Reds might move to New York. The New York Reds? The Brooklyn Reds? Not likely. It became clear in short order that Crosley was using the threat of a move to New York to get taxpayer-funded upgrades to Crosley Field, especially to gain more parking lots. Crosley Field had a seating capacity of roughly 29,000, and parking was severely restricted. Improved parking could lead to increased revenue and a better ball club than the fourth-place team of 1957. As has so often happened with such threats to move in other cities, city officials in Cincinnati hastened to ante up, in this case, by providing 2,800 additional parking spaces. They also began talking of building a new riverfront stadium. These moves led Crosley to announce that he would stay in Cincinnati, which is, of course, what he had planned to do anyway.

By the middle of 1958, Shea's efforts had availed him nothing—nothing that is to say, in the way of a Major League commitment to move a team to New York. He had tried Pittsburgh, Philadelphia, and Cincinnati. He had met with owners at the All-Star Game in July 1958, on that occasion with an ace up his sleeve: the city of New York was going to support construction of a new stadium in Flushing Meadows. He also knew, because baseball's commissioner, Ford Frick, had told him so, that the move of the Giants and the Dodgers to the West Coast did not mean that the territorial rights to all of New York City devolved to the Yankees. The National League still had territorial rights for one and perhaps two clubs in the city. That Frick did not have as much authority over such things—or any other important baseball matter—as he seemed to imply, had not yet dawned on Shea. But Shea left the All-Star Game disheartened. National League president Warren Giles told him pretty directly that no team would move to New York, certainly not in the immediate future.[4]

Shea was disheartened but not deterred. He had been talking to Branch Rickey, who advised him that since the National League had no interest in moving a team to New York, the only logical thing to do was start a new league with a team in the city. In fact, in Rickey's opinion it was time for expansion, and to him the only logical way to expand was with an entirely new league. Shea subsequently held a news conference on November 12, 1958, at Toots Shor's restaurant in which he announced that his committee had decided on "a new task." This new task would be a third Major League. He hoped that Major League Baseball would accept the new league and bring it under the auspices of Organized Baseball. But if that were not the case, his new league would operate independently. He had ownership groups lined up, he stated a bit prematurely, in enough cities; and it was entirely possible that a team would be playing in New York during the 1960 season. Ford Frick had not been consulted, however, and he was not pleased. Over the next year and a half, he and the presidents of the National and American Leagues worked assiduously to thwart Shea's and Rickey's plans.

As early as 1953 Rickey had begun thinking of the third-league mode of expansion; not long after his dismissal by the Pirates he began to consider it in a more focused manner. In an article in the *Sporting News* on May 21, 1958, a front-page piece, he made his case: "The time is ripe for the majors to expand," he declared, and "expansion should be the creation of the present two leagues." There should not be a war as had occurred with the founding of the American League or with the beginning of the ill-fated Federal League of 1914 and 1915, but if the National and American Leagues refused to cooperate, then a war might become necessary. "A third major," he continued, "is something we must have soon." Rickey firmly believed that a new eight-team league, with talent fairly equally distributed among the teams, would be competitive, attract fans, and make money. If the established leagues simply added a team or two, however, the result would be losing records, last-place finishes for the new teams, and poor attendance. A third league, he insisted, was the only way to expand. Ironically, Taylor Spink, who as editor of the *Sporting News* seemed to put his imprimatur on Rickey's ideas, would soon become a staunch opponent of the third league.[5]

Branch Rickey was a thundering paradox of a man: as a devout Methodist, he did not drink, swear, or go to the ballpark on Sunday; he was a civil rights leader who not only integrated Major League Baseball but also despised and railed against injustice inflicted on African Americans. He was, simultaneously, a sharp businessman who often paid his players less than a living wage, showed no qualms about cheating a rival in a player deal, and, most especially, never blinked when it came to dealing in human flesh—indeed he profited enormously from the sale of players. (Of such sales and trades he always said he was selling and trading contracts, not players!)

It became apparent before long that it was Branch Rickey, not Bill Shea, who had taken the lead toward establishing a third Major League. And Rickey, despite his age and infirmities connected with it, was a formidable figure not to be taken lightly. Born in south central Ohio in the small farming village of Stockdale, near Lucasville, in 1881, Rickey had attended Ohio Wesleyan University, where for two years he played football and baseball. Because he had taken money to play semiprofessional baseball for a team in Portsmouth, Ohio, in the summer of 1902, he was declared ineligible to play either baseball or football during his last two years at Ohio Wesleyan. But he was asked to coach the baseball team, an assignment he completed successfully. In the summers after his third and fourth years in college, he played professional baseball as a catcher, first for LaMars, Iowa, in the Iowa-Dakota League, then for Dallas in the Texas League, and for the Cincinnati Reds of the National League. The latter team released him near the end of the 1904 season, after he had played in only a few exhibition and no regular-season games. The Reds' manager did not want to carry, understandably, a catcher who would not play on Sundays.

In the fall of 1904, Rickey accepted a teaching position for 1904–5 at Allegheny College in Meadville, Pennsylvania, where he would also coach the baseball and football teams. Then in the summer of 1905 he went again to the Major Leagues with the St. Louis Browns, followed by a demotion later in the season, once again to Dallas. In 1906 he was back with the Browns, with a second job lined up for the fall and spring semesters as basketball, football, and baseball coach at Ohio Wesleyan. In 1906 he also completed his BA at the school and married the woman who would become his lifetime partner and the mother of his six children, Jane Moulton.

Although he looked forward to the 1907 season with the Browns, over the winter he developed a sore arm that concerned him and led him to wonder if he could compete successfully. In the spring of 1907, the Browns sold him outright to the New York Highlanders, where he achieved a catching record that remained unbroken over a hundred years later: he gave up thirteen consecutive stolen bases in a single game loss to the Washington Senators. That was not the end of his playing career, but almost. Clearly he could no longer throw effectively.

A bout with tuberculosis in the intervening years and his continuing work at Ohio Wesleyan slowed his progress toward a permanent, more respectable career than baseball. But in 1910 he enrolled in the University of Michigan law school, where he completed the three-year degree in two. While at Michigan he also coached the baseball team, an assignment he carried out so successfully he was kept on for the 1912 and 1913 seasons.

In 1913 he returned to the Major Leagues, beginning a career that would make him a business manager, a field manager, a general manager, and, overall, one of the most successful executives in the history of the game. Between 1913 and 1955, he held the following positions: business manager of the St. Louis Browns and field manager from 1913 through 1915; assistant to the owner of the Browns in 1916; president and part owner of the St. Louis Cardinals from 1917 to 1919; field manager of the Cardinals from 1919 to 1925; general manager of the Cardinals from 1925 to 1942; general manager of the Brooklyn Dodgers from 1942 to 1950; and general manager of the Pittsburgh Pirates from 1950 to 1955. In all these positions from 1925 onward, regardless of his ancillary titles, he was always the general manager, the chief evaluator of talent and a major force in running the ball clubs.

Rickey's contributions to baseball were numerous and significant. He started the St. Louis Cardinals farm system, which became a prototype for all others to follow and a system that saw the Cardinals gain ownership of dozens of Minor League ball clubs. By the late 1930s the Cardinals "owned" or controlled over seven hundred players and either owned outright or had working agreements with more than thirty clubs. In 1938 and 1939 respectively there were twenty-one and twenty-two D-classification leagues in Organized Baseball. The Cardinals owned or had working agreements with a ball club in each one of them. (A working agreement meant that in return for a subsidy from the Cardinals, a Minor League club would take some, maybe an entire roster, of young Cardinal players; those players, whom the Minor League club might "own" outright, the

Cardinals could, if they wished, acquire for the following season.) Rickey's Cardinal farm system was so extensive that several clubs in a given league might find themselves using players signed by St. Louis. The system conformed with Rickey's view that there was quality in quantity. Players he did not need he sold, often for handsome prices, and he personally kept 10 percent of the sale price. To supply the farm system, Rickey used tryout camps, which hundreds of players attended across the country. At these camps Rickey's scouts, or Rickey himself, evaluated a player's running speed, strength of throwing arm, hitting power, softness of hands, quickness of feet, and general baseball instincts.

Rickey's ball clubs, certainly during spring training, went to school on his ideas. He used sliding pits to teach players to hook slide to the right and to the left. He set up batting cages with pitching machines to give hitters repetitive practice in perfecting their swings. He taught hitters to hold their bats off the shoulder, and back, to generate power. He expounded on the hit and run; he was not fond of the play. He lectured pitchers on the bad things that could happen if they threw sliders; he did not like the effect the pitch had on their arms or how it diminished the break on their curve balls. He preached "get hold of a seam" to all fielders when making throws. And on and on. Nothing escaped him.

He built winning ball clubs in St. Louis and Brooklyn; and in Brooklyn he made his greatest contribution to baseball and to American life in the signing of Jackie Robinson. Robinson and Rickey became legitimate heroes of the civil rights movement. Robinson helped the Dodgers win five pennants as well. Except for his field managerial experience with the Browns and then the Cardinals, Rickey was a huge success—until he went to Pittsburgh.

Outmaneuvered for control of the Dodgers by Walter O'Malley, Rickey signed on as the Pirates' general manager in 1950. Pittsburgh had a star player in home run hitter Ralph Kiner, but not much else. The Pirates were a perennially losing club. In 1948 they had finished fourth not far behind the Boston Braves, who had won the pennant. After that their performances put them at or near the bottom of the league. They had little operating money, and their Minor League cupboard was bare. Rickey could not bring a winner to Pittsburgh, and he was released in 1955. When the Pirates won in 1960, apologists for Rickey were quick to point out that it was he who had signed Dick Groat, Bob Skinner, Roberto Clemente, Elroy Face, Bill Mazeroski, and other stars of the 1960 team. That was certainly true, but fairness requires pointing out that it was also Rickey who had signed Tony Bartirome, Bobby Del Greco, Jack Merson, Clem Koshorek, Johnny and Eddie O'Brien, Vic Janowitz— and for a bonus exceeding what the Yankees gave Mickey Mantle, Mario Cuomo. It was Rickey who had fielded a team in 1952 that won 42 games and lost 112, arguably the worst team in baseball history, certainly one of the worst. Many of the players on that team were barely out of high school and were paid the Major League minimum salary of five thousand dollars per year. Fans who followed that team wondered how they managed to win forty-two games. Rickey's Pirate team in 1955 drew only 469,000 fans.[6]

Rickey was old, had heart trouble and Meniere's disease, and he had failed in his latest baseball endeavor. But he was not ready to give up, or retire, when he met up with Bill Shea. Shea had been in touch with Ford Frick, who, unlike Warren Giles, seemed to favor expansion. But Frick, though a likable man, a former sportswriter, was not a leader or a man of intellectual depth. Then in his midsixties, he was not prepared to resist the pressures of the owners. When the owners heard of Shea's talk of a third league, they bristled. When the owners bristled, Frick bristled. He announced that he would not be pressured into putting a new team in New York, through either the relocation of an existing team or a third-league team. And where, Frick suggested, did Shea get off thinking he could bring a third league into Organized Baseball without the commissioner's approval?[7]

The third league would face four major obstacles: gaining dynamic leadership roughly equivalent to that of Ban Johnson; keeping the new ownership groups on board and in line; gaining the approval of Organized Baseball's establishment; and identifying players who could qualify as Major Leaguers. These hurdles were in addition to the challenge of bringing in enough new teams. In the spring and summer of 1959, five team ownership groups quickly emerged in New York, Toronto, Houston, Denver, and Minneapolis.

The group in New York included Herbert Walker, the wealthy uncle of George Herbert Walker Bush; Dwight Davis, a man of even greater means, whose name is associated with tennis's Davis Cup, named for his father; Dorothy Killam, part owner of a Brooklyn newspaper and wife of a wealthy Canadian lumberman—a woman who Rickey told Ford Frick had at her disposal $135 million in cash. Unable to continue as part of the group, she gave way to Joan Payson, the sister of John Whitney, the U.S. ambassador to Great Britain, who had made much of his wealth as publisher of the *New York Herald Tribune*. Mrs. Payson, as heir to the Whitney fortune and partner of Donald Grant, a wealthy banker, was at least as well healed as Mrs. Killam. She had served on the board of the New York Giants and tried to buy the team rather than have Horace

Stoneham take it to San Francisco. She later became owner of the expansion New York Mets of the National League.[8]

In Toronto the forty-seven-year-old Jack Kent Cooke took the lead. As a young man Cooke had been a prodigy in several areas of endeavor. He was an accomplished musician, a saxophonist in the Canadian touring band of Percy Faith. He was a brilliant hockey player, good enough for the University of Michigan to offer him a scholarship. Like so many young men of the Depression era, he decided to eschew college and move on to the world of work—at whatever job he could earn a decent income. He quickly learned that he could indeed earn more than a decent income, as his entrepreneurial talents led him to ownership of a Toronto radio station and the *New Liberty* magazine. In the late 1940s he bought the Toronto Maple Leafs hockey team and then in 1951 became owner of the Toronto Minor League Baseball club in the International League. He came into baseball as he had into other enterprises: at the right time. Minor League attendance was booming in the late forties and early fifties, a phenomenon Cooke abetted with sparkling, pennant-winning ball clubs in 1954, 1956, and 1957. In 1954 his International League club drew over four hundred thousand fans, and in 1956 and 1957 well over three hundred thousand. He had failed in repeated efforts to bring a Major League team to Toronto, a city of approximately 1.3 million people in the late 1950s, because Major League owners thought cold weather in the spring and fall would keep fans away. So he was eager to join the third league.[9]

Baseball has attracted some interesting characters over its long history, none more flamboyant, colorful, and sometimes disagreeable than the leading figure in Houston's third-league effort, George Kirksey. Born in the smallish central

THE CONTINENTAL LEAGUE CONCEIVED

Texas town of Hillsboro, where his parents ran a boardinghouse, he went on to a career in sportswriting, public relations, and self-promotion. Though he had completed only two years at the University of Texas and was not highly educated in a formal sense, he lacked nothing in self-confidence or willingness to inform others of their stupidity. A tall, thin, and not unattractive man, he married the big-band singer Ethel Shutta, a union not made in heaven. He went through people, and wives, and was easily bored, but he was good at drawing attention to himself and his ideas. In the 1920s, 1930s, and early 1940s, he wrote feature stories for *Colliers*, *Look*, and *Saturday Evening Post* while also writing sports for United Press in Chicago and New York. His assignments included covering twelve World Series, six Sugar Bowls, and six Rose Bowls. During World War II he served as the chief public relations officer of the Air Corps in Europe, so in 1946 when he arrived in Houston, he was well known.

Kirksey believed Houston, which had doubled in population since 1930, should be a Major League town. To that end he began making contact with the seriously moneyed oilmen of the city, most notably R. E. "Bob" Smith, whose stationery was said to have read simply "Oil Operator," and Craig Cullinan. Smith pledged $250,000 to buy the Philadelphia Athletics on the premise that nine other investors would join in making the $2.5 million deal. The Athletics, with the blessing and connivance of the New York Yankees and the Yankees' close ties to Kansas City businessman Arnold Johnson, went to Kansas City instead. Kirksey in turn tried to lure the Cardinals, the Reds, and the Senators to Houston, all to no avail.

In January 1957 Kirksey brought thirty-five of Houston's wealthiest, most prominent men together to form the

Houston Sports Authority. Its mission was to bring a Major League Baseball team to the city and to lobby the Harris County Parks Commission to authorize a new stadium. Kirksey was not a self-effacing man, but he did not seek the presidency of the Sports Authority, instead urging his friend and associate Craig Cullinan to do the job. Cullinan was the offspring of a wealthy oilman who had moved to Texas from Pennsylvania, the founder of the Texaco Company. Young Cullinan had gone off to Andover and Yale and then returned to Houston to work in the family business. His personality was far different from that of Kirksey; he was a quiet, shy man, but a person whose wealth carried clout, someone who could get things done. Working together Kirksey and Cullinan had no trouble persuading the board of park commissioners to recommend a new stadium—a grandiose, domed edifice that would sit on five hundred acres with enormous parking lots, and host not only baseball but football, other sports, and entertainment events. When Cullinan and Kirksey met Rickey, they were enthralled; and Rickey, as an old farm boy, was taken by Kirksey's life story, not to mention his enthusiasm.[10]

Another ownership group for Rickey's new league was put together in Denver, led by forty-one-year-old Robert Lee "Bob" Howsam, son of a southern Colorado farmer, himself a farmer and beekeeper in southern Colorado. More importantly, Howsam had been a student at the University of Colorado, where he met and eventually married the daughter of prominent Colorado politician Edwin Carl "Big Ed" Johnson. Johnson took a keen interest in Howsam, who had been a high school football and baseball player, saw him as a talented and appropriate mate for his daughter, and in 1947 hired him as his administrative assistant. Johnson, then serving in the U.S. Senate had been governor of Colorado, then a three-term U.S. senator, and would eventually serve as governor again. He also loved baseball but was a staunch opponent of the monopolistic practices in Organized Baseball. After Howsam married Johnson's daughter, Johnson hired Howsam to run the Western League, a Class A Minor League that Johnson himself had supervised as voluntary president from 1945 to 1958.

Before long Howsam was a rising figure in the baseball ranks, and with Johnson's help, he gained ownership of the Denver ball club in the Western League, where his efforts won him, in 1951 and again in 1956, the *Sporting News* honor as Minor League executive of the year. In 1956 the Class A Denver Bears became the Triple-A Denver Bears, because after the Athletics moved from Philadelphia to Kansas City, the Triple-A Kansas City Blues had to move. Howsam bought the Blues for ninety thousand dollars and brought them to Denver as an American Association franchise. When Howsam, after several years of successful operation of the Denver club, heard of the proposed third league, he met with Rickey and enthusiastically signed on as a charter member. He did so with "Big Ed's" blessing and promise of help, if needed, in the U.S. Congress.[11]

As the winter of 1959 gave way to spring and summer, the third league continued to take shape. Minneapolis-St. Paul, despite its often awful weather, had hosted thriving franchises in the American Association for many years. Both cities had ball clubs, and both historically drew good crowds, though attendance for each had dropped to about 150,000 in 1958. From the midfifties onward the Washington Senators had eyed the Twin Cities area as a possible relocation site. Longtime owner, ex-manager, and baseball executive Clark Griffith had died in 1955, leaving the Senators to his slow-witted, doughy-faced, penurious adopted son, Calvin, who spoke of, or hinted at, his desire to move the Senators to the Minneapolis area. Congress rebelled, forcing Calvin Griffith to back away from the move—and to continue his marginal operation in Washington, which included fielding decidedly bad ball clubs.

When it became apparent that young Griffith would face major obstacles in moving to Minnesota, a group of investors led by Wheelock Whitney, a young investment banker from St. Cloud, swung into action, hoping to gain a third-league franchise. The Twin Cities had already built a stadium in Bloomington—now the location of the Mall of America—that would need only modest remodeling to become Major League ready. Whitney, then thirty-three years of age, an Andover-Yale graduate and friend of Craig Cullinan, received pledges of financial support from the Dayton Department Store owners, executives of the Hamm Brewing Company, Pillsbury Mills, and the *Star Tribune* newspaper. The Twin Cities would become one of the five charter members of the new league.[12]

The third league now had five ownership groups ready to move forward but plenty of issues yet to address. One of the issues was a name. No one knew what to call the organization. Several possibilities surfaced, including "the Pan-Am League" and "the United States League." The former did not sound quite right. The latter would have been fine except that Toronto was in the league. "The Third League" was too simple. "Big Ed" Johnson had the answer: "the Continental League." It was a master stroke. The league might eventually span the continent. The name stuck.

The Continental League in the summer of 1959 had five franchises. It had an adviser and possible leader in Branch Rickey, who had been working with Bill Shea since early in the year. In February 1959 Rickey had written a kind of manifesto extolling the third-league mode of expansion and spelling out the need: more boys playing; the growth in the U.S. population; airplanes reducing travel times; and, most especially, fair competition within a new league. The new league was ready to go public. It had wealthy owners ready to start. On July 27, 1959, at the Biltmore Hotel in midtown Manhattan, Bill Shea stood before an assemblage of interested onlookers and eager newsmen to announce the birth of the third league.

Shea himself was the logical choice for president of the Continental League, but he refused and urged Branch Rickey to take the post. Rickey, then seventy-seven years of age (he would turn seventy-eight on December 20) and, as he put it, feeling his age, demurred, but only briefly. He had his chance at long last to do what his greatest hero in baseball, Ban Johnson, had done. Besides that everyone in baseball knew that Rickey had become the prime force in the move toward expansion.

There was one immediate complicating factor for Rickey, however. His old friend and Pittsburgh Pirates owner John Galbreath knew of his third-league connections and was not pleased. Galbreath reminded Rickey that he still owned Pirates stock and was on Galbreath's payroll. When Galbreath fired him in 1955, he had given Rickey a fifty-thousand-dollar salary as a consultant; it was a sinecure requiring no real duties. But Galbreath hated the notion of a third league and hoped to dissuade Rickey from leading it by reminding him of his duties, obligations, and loyalties. Rickey's consulting contract with the Pirates forbade his working for any other Major League team. When Rickey told Galbreath on July 27 that he planned to sell all his Pirates stock and quit the consulting job, the Pirates' owner tried to talk him out of it. Rickey recalled, "He [said that he] had stood by me from the time he first met me and that he felt that now there was a reciprocal relationship which should be maintained." Rickey's response was, "You fired me from my present job and you know it." Rickey sold his stock to Galbreath for two hundred thousand dollars.[13]

On August 18, 1959, at the Warwick Hotel in New York, Bill Shea introduced Rickey as the first president of the Continental League. As president Rickey could emulate Ban Johnson but with a major difference: when Johnson had organized the American League, he was thirty-six years old and in his prime. Rickey was past his prime and in precarious health. Neither age nor health, nor the bare-bones existence of the new league, however, could keep the old baseball man down, could keep him from moving forward. For a while he had no office; he was the office, until he could rent space on Fifth Avenue in Manhattan. He had no staff, but he quickly organized one consisting of Arthur Mann, who had worked for Rickey for years and would direct the public relations effort; Kenneth Blackburn, who had been his secretary in Pittsburgh; and two young women secretaries, Judy Wilpon and Margaret Regetz. George Kirksey hung around to help get things going, though his main interest was in promoting the Houston franchise. Rickey himself rented a suite in Sutton Place and commuted, whenever he could, back to his home in Pittsburgh. His salary was set at $4,166 per month—$49,992 per year—plus $416 per month for expenses, and the term of appointment was sixteen months. The limited term may have reflected either his optimism in getting the new league started or concern about his age.[14]

Office space and staff help were the least concerns of Continental League leadership. When Rickey became president, the league—destined, it was assumed, to become an eight-team organization—had only five cities on board. Through the remainder of the summer and into the fall of 1959, many of the critics, press critics in particular, but also the presidents of the National and American Leagues hammered the new league as one in name only, as a five-franchise fiction. In December 1959 and January 1960, the Continental League addressed this issue. Rickey wanted Atlanta in the league, if possible, and he wanted Earl Mann, the owner of the Atlanta Crackers of the Southern Association, to play a role in bringing it about. Mann was a longtime successful baseball person, a fixture in the Southern Association who had made that franchise into a model for Minor League Baseball. Just as important to Rickey, Mann had integrated the league in 1954, if only briefly, with the inclusion of outfielder Nat Peeples on the Atlanta roster. Rickey was also undoubtedly thinking ahead and hoping that Mann would help obviate the problem of territorial payments for Continental League access to Atlanta.

Mann was in trouble financially in 1959. I learned this firsthand in early May of that year, when Mann, acting on the recommendation of, in his words, a highly respected former player, manager, and scout, invited me to try out with the Crackers. He did not have in mind that I was ready to play in the Southern Association but that he might sign me for the Braves organization; Atlanta that year and since 1950 had a working agreement with the Boston and then Milwaukee Braves. After three days of workouts with the ball club in front of manager Buddy Bates and one of his coaches, Mann asked that I come into his office to discuss a contract. His office was a Spartan, almost forbidding, space in Ponce de Leon Park, the home of the Crackers. Following a casual, extremely amicable conversation, he offered me a contract for three hundred dollars a month to go to the Nebraska State League to play for McCook. I reminded him that I was no longer a rookie and had been in that league two years before. His response was that the manager at McCook, Bill Steinecke, would arrange to send me to one of the other Braves clubs, that the Braves would find a place for me somewhere in the organization. I then asked for a five-hundred-dollar bonus, because I needed some new baseball shoes and two new gloves—a first baseman's mitt and an outfielder's glove. He then told me that times were tough, and he was losing money, but that if I signed he would make sure that I got the equipment I had requested, presumably through a subvention from the Braves. Mann struck me as a genuinely nice and decent man, one of the best people I had met in baseball, but I decided to sign the following week with the Washington organization.

Mann was indeed losing money. During my brief time in Atlanta, during which the Crackers were playing Mobile, one of the top clubs in the league, I saw only a few hundred people each night at the ballpark—and they had good reason to stay away. The Crackers were not a good ball club. They ended the season drawing only slightly over 71,000 fans to watch a team that finished last, thirty-five games out of first place. Mann later told Rickey that he had lost one hundred thousand dollars in 1959 and was in no position to become part of an Atlanta ownership group. Undaunted, Rickey offered Mann the position of general manager of the New York club and turned to F. Eaton Chalkley to head up ownership in Atlanta. Chalkley had made his money as a developer of shopping malls and had married Susan Hayward, the famous actress, who could tide him over in a pinch.[15]

Two other franchises rounded out the league. Dallas-Fort Worth got one of them, the ownership led by Amon Carter, publisher of the *Dallas-Fort Worth Telegram*, and millionaire construction businessman J. R. Bateson, with Lamar Hunt, son of megamillionaire oilman H. L. Hunt, on the board. In January the new league completed its eight-team organization with the addition of Buffalo. John Stiglmeir, a wealthy businessman, led the ownership there. Buffalo was an excellent baseball city; four hundred thousand fans had turned out to watch the Buffalo club win the International League pennant in 1959.[16]

Finishing the Continental League roster of teams gave the leadership a lift at the end of the year and gave Branch Rickey pleasure at the nervousness evoked from Walter O'Malley. The Hollywood Stars and the Los Angeles Angels of the Pacific Coast League had been fixtures in that league and had shared the Los Angeles market for years. After O'Malley moved the Dodgers to Los Angeles, territory, incidentally, that became his for a song, the Angels moved to Spokane and the Stars to Salt Lake City. Former officials and board members of the Hollywood club lamented its move: actors Dean Martin, Jack Webb, and, most especially, Chuck Connors, who had been a Brooklyn Dodgers Minor League player and briefly a Major Leaguer with the Dodgers and the Cubs. (In 1959 Connors was the star of the hit television show *The Rifleman*.) These dignitaries and Stars' broadcaster, Mark Scott, saw in the Continental League a chance to have two Major League teams in Los Angeles, to have "continuous baseball," as Scott put it. Scott went to see O'Malley in mid-October, not long after the Dodgers' victory over the Chicago White Sox in the World Series, to tell the Dodgers' owner that another Major League team was coming to Los Angeles—from the Continental League. Scott reported to Rickey that O'Malley was very upset by the news, even more upset at Scott's suggestion that the new team, for a rental fee, would like to play in the Dodgers new stadium when the Dodgers were on the road. O'Malley, in Scott's words, "was totally shocked" and "demanded to know who the persons were" behind the Continental League and its potential move to Los Angeles. Anyone this side of the moon, including O'Malley, knew it was Branch Rickey. Rickey, though he informed Scott that the new league did not at that time have Los Angeles in mind, followed up with O'Malley. On January 15, 1960, he wrote the Dodgers' owner, "It could be, and may be, that you do not object to sharing, for a satisfactory price, the nation's third largest city to make possible continuous baseball. I do not know your answer."[17]

Rickey, whose contempt for O'Malley was palpable and nearly unbounded, had stuck in the knife, had made his old opponent squirm. In early November 1959, not long after Scott's overture to O'Malley and O'Malley's feigned ignorance of the power behind the Continental League, Rickey confided his thoughts to his new league associates; "Walter O'Malley," he said, "has become huge and fat" and talked behind everyone's back. He was a classic double-dealer, was never to be trusted, and was "strong for anybody so long he [could] use them—if they [could] really help O'Malley." Otherwise, he was "positively ruthless."[18]

But by 1960 the Continental League did not need Los Angeles, or at least not yet. League officials had other concerns dating to July and August 1959. Rickey and Bill Shea clearly wanted the imprimatur of Organized Baseball and did not at that time wish to be considered an outlaw organization. Former senator and league backer Ed Johnson of Colorado was not nearly as charitable toward the lords of the existing leagues as Rickey and hoped to see a legislative challenge to them. That challenge had a remote chance of success in July, when Senator Estes Kefauver of Tennessee, a member of the Judiciary Committee and chairman of the Senate Judiciary Subcommittee on Antitrust and Monopoly, held hearings on baseball and bills recently introduced to address its antitrust exemption. Kefauver had made a name for himself in several respects: for his overweaning ego, his hearings on organized crime, his run for the Democratic nomination for the presidency in 1952 (he became Adlai Stevenson's running mate in 1956), and his genuinely progressive views on monopoly. He had been a football player at the University of Tennessee but had shown no great interest in baseball—except to note the monopolistic practices of the sport. In that he was advised daily by his chief counsel and assistant, Rand Dixon. Dixon, correctly as it turned out, did not believe the existing ownership would cooperate with a third league.

Rickey made a presentation to Kefauver's committee. Wearing his customary bow tie, chewing on a cigar, and propping himself up with a cane, which he periodically thumped on the table for emphasis, the old baseball man made a case to Kefauver's committee that was really aimed primarily at conciliating the baseball establishment, of which he had until so recently been a part: "Do you think that Gus Busch, Powell Crosley, John Galbreath, my good friend Wrigley, or Mr. Yawkey, or Del Webb, oh, it is unkind not to include them all, that they are that definition of sportsmen who would for forty years do phony deals in the transaction of players' contracts and continue to do it? And maintain their self-respect in their own communities, which they do enjoy? That is unthinkable. It isn't true."[19]

Of course, it was true. "Big Ed" Johnson knew it was true. Representative Emmanuel Celler of Brooklyn knew it was true. Senator Kenneth Keating of New York knew it was true. Kefauver knew it was true. Most players knew it was true. Rickey himself knew it was true. He had been, after all, one of them. For now, however, as he was about to accept the presidency of the Continental League, he wanted, he needed, the cooperation of the National and the American League owners.

What Rickey wanted most, though he did not say it, was to avoid the experience of the Federal League. The Federal League had its origins in 1913 as an independent circuit that operated outside the structure of Organized Baseball and relied on the services of semiprofessional or amateur players to fill its teams' rosters. During the winter of 1913–14, the league president, James Gilmore of Chicago, sought to join the National Agreement of 1903—then the governing agreement of Organized Baseball and the peace treaty between the National and the American League—as a third Major League. The Federal League would, in Gilmore's words, abide by all the requirements of the agreement and subject itself to the governing commission, a three-member body consisting of the presidents of the National and American Leagues and an elected chairman. Ban Johnson, by 1914 arguably the most powerful figure in Major League Baseball, refused the entreaties of the new league. He believed, probably erroneously, that the two eight-team leagues already consumed the nation's best available talent; a third league would spread the talent too thin.

Rebuffed in their plea to join Organized Baseball, the Federal League owners decided to move forward on their own. They branded the existing baseball structure a monopoly and called the reserve clause, in existence in one form or another since 1879, illegal and wholly inoperative. They then set out to sign as many existing Major League players as they could get for, at the time, handsome salaries. Some prominent players jumped to the new league, most notably Hal Chase of the Chicago White Sox, Charles "Chief" Bender and Eddie Plank of the Philadelphia Athletics, George Stovall from the St. Louis Browns, and Mordecai "Three Finger" Brown of the Chicago Cubs. Most of the big stars stayed put, largely because National and American League clubs raised their salaries dramatically (only to lower them again after the Federal League's demise), and John McGraw, manager of the New York Giants, turned down a one-hundred-thousand-dollar offer to manage in the new league. Over one hundred high-classification Minor Leaguers joined the circuit in an exodus that had special meaning for those owners faced with the Continental League challenge.

When National and American League owners sued the Federal League clubs in state courts to prevent their executing contracts with reserved players, the Federal League countered with a suit in the Federal District Court of Northern Illinois under the Sherman and Clayton antitrust acts, challenging the reserve clause and Organized Baseball's monopoly. A federal judge in Michigan had already ruled in early 1914 that the reserve clause was illegal.

Unfortunately for the Federal League, the presiding judge in northern Illinois, Kenesaw Mountain Landis, a baseball fan of the Chicago Cubs prejudiced in favor of the existing structure of baseball and later baseball commissioner, sat on the case. He refused to make a ruling in the hope that eventually Federal League losses would lead to an accommodation with Organized Baseball. Michael Shapiro has offered a brilliant and insightful portrait of Landis: "Landis looked like everything he was not: restrained, prudent, and wise. He had a great shock of white hair and a well-lined face that appeared incapable of a smile—the very picture of a judge, biblically speaking."[20]

The result of Landis's action, or inaction, was an agreement in December 1915 in which the National and the American League clubs bought out the Federal League owners for six hundred thousand dollars to be spread among the eight teams and gained the right to purchase Federal League players. This was not a bad deal for those Federal League clubs that had lost money, though several of them had made some money in 1914. A prime reason for the deal was that some of the Federal League owners, especially Charlie Weeghman of the Chicago Whales, who made his money with a string of restaurants and built Wrigley Field, worked almost from the beginning to swing a deal (a sellout) with the established clubs of Organized Baseball. He hoped to gain respectability by joining the elite club. This situation was not lost on Branch Rickey in 1959 and 1960, as he struggled to keep Continental League owners on board.

At any rate, because they were blocked in an attempt to buy the St. Louis Cardinals and move them to Baltimore, the Baltimore Federal League owners filed an antitrust suit in U.S. District Court in Washington DC in September 1917 against Organized Baseball. This case resulted, in 1922, in the U.S. Supreme Court's ruling exempting Organized Baseball from antitrust legislation. The court's ruling meant that not only could Organized Baseball continue using the reserve clause, but it could also continue awarding exclusive, monopolistic, territorial rights to clubs within Organized Baseball—a practice begun in 1876 with the advent of the National League.[21]

Rickey and Shea in particular wanted to avoid Federal League defections, its "outlaw" reputation, and its ultimate failure as a viable organization. Immediately following the August 18 Warwick Hotel announcement of Rickey's presidency of the Continental League, Rickey, Shea, George

Kirksey, and Jack Kent Cooke of the Toronto franchise met with representatives of the National and the American Leagues at Ford Frick's office at Rockefeller Center. Twenty-two people in all attended this important meeting, which Frick himself considered cordial. Frick emphasized afterward that he favored expansion and did not oppose the third-league mode of carrying it out, as long as the new league met the requirements that Major League Baseball had laid down earlier. His disingenuousness was palpable but not then fully evident.[22]

In 1958, after the Giants and the Dodgers moved to the West Coast, the owners began considering how they would deal with possible pressure from Congress to take Major League Baseball to more American cities. Hence they drafted a set of rules for expansion. If a new league was added—the thought initially and for several years prior to 1958 was of possible Major League status for the Pacific Coast League, which for a time operated with "open classification" status—that league would have to include eight teams; provide full data on finances; have an aggregate population of 15 million; contain ballparks with at least 25,000 seating capacity; demonstrate aggregate attendance over three years of 2.5 million; play a balanced schedule of 154 games; accept the Major League minimum salary; accept all other terms of the Major League rules on player contracts; participate in the pension plan; and apply for Major League standing six months in advance. Only part of this seemed a problem to the wealthy Continental League executives. But as soon became clear, the National and the American Leagues themselves accepted none of these conditions and would in fact work assiduously to undercut the third-league form of expansion.[23]

Why would the existing Major League owners become so resistant, so quickly, to the Continental League? There were several reasons, some of them social, cultural, and racially informed—to be addressed later—some of them financially selfish or venal. One such reason was pay television. Bill Shea came to understand early on that National and American League owners were beginning to envision the huge profits possible through pay TV. They had in mind the division of the receipts sixteen ways and not twenty-four. They were doubtful, at the same time, that new league teams would contribute much to the pot.

Pay television as a forerunner to the cable television of a later generation was a new thing in the 1950s—a way for aspiring entrepreneurs to make serious money off the new medium. In 1946 there were 6,400 television sets in the United States; by 1956 there were 40 million. As early as 1951 communication firms in Chicago and Los Angeles were, on a limited basis, providing pay television service for movies. The movies were more expensive in home than in the theater, but viewers were apparently willing to pay for the convenience. Pollsters for *Television Age* in 1957 did a survey of eight hundred families in New York and found that over 40 percent of them would be willing to pay to watch baseball on TV. If, the pollsters concluded, there were 346,000 television sets wired for pay service and the owners of the sets paid only twenty-five cents per game, the Brooklyn Dodgers would make over eighty-six thousand dollars per game. For a full season, then a seventy-seven-game home schedule, they would earn nearly nine million dollars, not counting what they might share in other markets as the visiting team. Owners could barely contain their excitement at the thought of their revenues if they could charge a dollar or two per game. All this, Shea knew, Rickey knew, Ford Frick knew, represented a potential bonanza to the established Major Leagues.[24]

How to gain acceptance within the existing structure of the Major Leagues, given the possible pay TV revenue and other disincentives for the National and American League clubs, would be a serious challenge for the Continental League leaders. Not only was the new league devoid of leverage, but the National and American Leagues held, or seemingly held, all the cards.

3

The Horsehide Cartel Challenged

Beginning in the summer of 1959, especially after Rickey's appointment as Continental League president, the leaders of Major League Baseball began acting like a boxer taking on an inferior opponent, an opponent perhaps incapable of winning the fight but nonetheless capable of inflicting serious damage. They bobbed and weaved, feigned this way and that, danced around, shot some left jabs, and occasionally threw a right-hand body blow. Ford Frick and his supporters at first implied that they would welcome a new league. Then they warned of difficulties. They cautioned Rickey about the costs of moving into established territories. They told him that his league would surely sell an inferior product. They hinted at placing National and American League teams in Continental League cities. Most of all, they talked, humored, and delayed, hoping that the new league would go away or that Congress might legislate it away.

On August 18, the day of his appointment, Rickey told the leaders of the Major Leagues: "We want your cooperation; we need your cooperation; we demand your cooperation."[1] But despite the amicable spirit apparent at that meeting, the established owners would not remain cooperative—or not for long. Troubles multiplied for the Continental League.

Rickey got word that Brooklyn's representative on the New York Board of Estimates wanted funds spent on a remodeled Ebbets Field rather than on a stadium in Flushing Meadows. The new Flushing Meadows ballpark was essential for the very existence of the Continental League. Other new Continental owners including George Kirksey began telling Rickey that Houston's investors, responding to sportswriters' columns questioning the possibilities for the new league, were growing restive. Ford Frick, swayed by the owners, began voicing doubts about the new league, especially about franchises that proposed to move into existing Minor League cities—which was all of them but New York. Would Continental League leaders agree to pay the Minor League club owners their asking prices for territorial rights?

Following the 1959 World Series, Calvin Griffith, the owner of the Washington Senators, announced that he hoped to move his team to Minneapolis. He had word, he said, that Minneapolis had investors lined up to bring the Senators to the Twin Cities, and he hoped to get the approval of Major League owners for the move. This announcement brought two significant developments: word from Major League owners, who feared the wrath of Congress and the removal of the antitrust exemption if the Senators left Washington, that they would not approve Griffith's proposed move; and more ominous for Continental League leaders, indication that the Minneapolis backers of the Continental League had applied to get an American League club. Bill Shea's response, in anger, was that the Twin Cities might get no franchise at all, either from the American or the Continental League.[2]

A corollary to the application of Minneapolis to join the American League was an announcement by Joe Cronin, president of the American League, that he was forming a committee to consider the possibility of expansion.

Cronin, then fifty-three years of age, beefy, thick necked, and paunchy, had been a star shortstop with Pittsburgh, Washington, and Boston, a former manager of the latter two clubs, whose defensive play was always deficient but whose bat—and connections—took him to the Hall of Fame in 1956. (He once made sixty-two errors in one season but he hit .301 lifetime.) As president he was always in the firm grip of the American League owners.

Rickey led the response to the challenges. He sent Cronin a sharply worded, hand-delivered letter on November 9, indicating that he knew of Cronin's appointment of a committee, consisting of baseball executives George Weiss, William O. DeWitt, and Henry B. Greenberg, to explore expansion of the American League to nine or ten teams. The purpose, Rickey said, was to encourage some Continental League cities to believe that they might be added to the American League for the 1960 season. This, Rickey told Cronin, was arrant foolishness, designed "for obstructing the organizational time table of the Continental League." He then asked the American League president and his committee to meet with various owners of the Continental League in their own cities and to do so before the month was out; the Continental League would pay all expenses incurred.[3]

The message to Cronin brought a telephone response from Commissioner Frick within minutes of its delivery—a response not unlike that of an angry bull to a red flag. Frick sensed in Rickey's comments a prospective war, and he did not want a war. A war, like the one with the Federal League, would bring salary competition, territorial challenges, and, without question, new legal challenges for baseball that would leave the national pastime battered and bruised, if not broken. Frick said to Rickey: "You think one way and I think another. I think we should sit down and talk this thing through. I know damned well the point you have in mind and so do you." His anger growing, the commissioner then warned: "I don't want this thing to go haywire." Rickey quickly recovered from his puzzled reaction and then told his colleagues, "At long last we have the Baseball Commissioner calling us." And it appeared that "the Commissioner [was] now ready to take a position on internal expansion. The whole idea [was] to defeat the Continental League."[4]

If Rickey knew Frick's intention about things "going haywire," he feigned ignorance. He asked Frick for a meeting: "How about today?" Frick was busy. "How about tomorrow?" Frick had a physical exam. "How about the 11th?" That was impossible because it was Veteran's Day. He needed time to work on a strategy to undercut the upstart league.[5] Most especially, Frick was worried about the possible limitations on the reserve clause. The Continental League would eventually get players, would develop them, but in an immediate sense it would want access to some of the roughly 4,200 players that the National and the American Leagues controlled. Upon reflection Rickey knew this was the main issue with Frick.

On November 10 Rickey had a phone conversation with Joe Cronin, whose job was to cajole the old baseball man, to humor him, and perhaps get him to rethink the new league. Rickey's account is noteworthy: "I have never heard such solicitude . . . about my knee, my heart, my wife, my children, my present, my past, my future." Cronin admitted that the American League was considering putting a ninth team in Minneapolis; he would let Rickey know something definite after December 7. Rickey responded a few days later, admonishing Cronin for meddling in Continental League territory for the sole purpose of sowing indecision in Continental League cities, for the sole purpose of undercutting the new league. "Surely Joe," Rickey noted, "you . . . know about the many telephone calls made by American League club officials in their alleged attempt to bring about a silly nine-club league."[6] A nine-club league, among other things, would create a scheduling nightmare.

Cronin may have been bluffing about internal expansion, but Rickey did not know—not, in any event for certain. But internal expansion by one or, more logically, two teams, which the American League constitution permitted, was not in itself a bar to Continental League success. Rickey told Cronin: "If you are going to expand by two teams name the cities and do it." Then the new league could go ahead with replacement cities, if necessary. "We must regard any further delay in revealing your expansion plans," Rickey continued, "as additional evidence that you share Commissioner Frick's opposition to the completion of the Continental League."[7] Cronin followed this message with further stalling; he could tell Rickey nothing except that expansion "must be carefully considered and not in haste." He did not say so, but his bosses, the American League owners, and especially the Yankees' owners, prevented his knowing or saying anything more. The Yankees wanted New York to themselves, and despite the commissioner's statement to the contrary, they began claiming exclusive territorial rights to the city. What they wanted and what they were pressuring Cronin and Frick to do was to use the possibility of internal expansion not as a prelude to actual expansion but as a way of killing the new league and keeping a new team out of New York.

If Rickey and his owners were worried in the fall of 1959, so were the National and the American Leagues. Rickey told Cronin in late November: "I must admit that the Commissioner's completely negative attitude toward a third major league has made an effective contribution to our forced delay and his continuous statement of preference for internal expansion hurts even more."[8] But the lords of Organized Baseball suffered disquiet as well. The National League was only lukewarm about internal expansion, largely because the most powerful owner, Walter O'Malley, did not see an imminent threat of invasion of his territory, despite a brief earlier scare, and hence was in no hurry to undercut the new league. American League owners knew they were in for an awful time from Congress if they allowed the Senators to move from Washington. All the Major League owners, though, knew that a new league would have not only new ballparks but a great chance at signing top talent, if for no other reason than players could expect a quicker rise to the Major Leagues through the Continental League route than with the more established leagues. And the owners knew that the Continental League would not be inferior for long.

How to defeat or circumvent the threat of internal expansion, or better put, how to proceed now that it appeared the Continental League would not be invited into the elite club, was the issue facing the founding members of the new league when they met near the end of November. Rickey readily admitted that he had been in error in his congressional testimony back in July extolling the generous and welcoming spirit of National and American League owners—in his belief that they would cooperate with the new league. "Big Ed" Johnson had been right; Rickey had been wrong. Now Rickey began to think that the way to proceed might be the way Ban Johnson had done in 1901: go independent, or "outlaw," the term so frequently used in 1901 and 1902 and again with the Federal League in 1914 and 1915. The mere threat of going independent might evoke cooperation from National and American League clubs. The

Continental League owners, however, were not anxious to proceed outside the confines of Organized Baseball. They preferred instead to follow Ed Johnson's advice and work with Congress, either to get a modification of baseball's exemption under the Sherman and Clayton antitrust laws or to get legislation limiting the number of players that teams could reserve.[9]

In the meantime Rickey and his owners began preparing for the winter baseball meetings scheduled for December in Miami. Before departing for Miami, Rickey received a letter from Walter O'Malley in which O'Malley said that prior to learning of the Continental League he had been in favor of adding an expansion club in each league. The National and the American Leagues would be divided into three six-team divisions. But now that he knew of the third league, that arrangement was not necessary. Oh, and by the way, regarding a team in Los Angeles, "I would like to know directly from you if your proposed league has such ambitions." He was still a bit nervous. Always wary of a possible démarche from O'Malley, Rickey said that the Continental League did not plan at that time to have a California club. Then he told his old adversary sharply: "The only reason I can possibly think of for the National League to expand to a ninth club would be to defeat the Continental League by placing a National League franchise in New York City."[10] At the meetings themselves Rickey, in his own words, "was covered by olive branches" and contacted by old friends and other baseball men wanting jobs in the new league. But he also learned that Organized Baseball officials remained unrelenting in their talk of internal expansion, that they persisted in what he saw as loose talk, or "charade," about cities that might get American or National League franchises: "The fictitious addition of one or two clubs, in any event, does not meet the need nor solve the problem." He left the meetings undaunted but less confident than ever about the immediate prospects for his new league. "The Continental League" he told a *New York Times* reporter, "is as inevitable as tomorrow, but not as imminent."[11]

Everything now depended on Congress. Why Congress? The answer is not simple and is only understandable in the context of the historic relationship of Organized Baseball and the courts. In the famous decision of 1922, Justice Oliver Wendell Holmes, writing for a unanimous Supreme Court, stated that while baseball teams crossed state lines to play games, their activity did not constitute interstate commerce in the strictest sense. Organized Baseball was thus not subject to the antitrust provisions of the Sherman and Clayton acts. Preposterous as this ruling seems in retrospect, it appears to have accorded with contemporary public sentiment and the justices' belief that the great national game required protection in the form of guaranteed territorial rights and continuation of the right to reserve players—as well as the arbitrary setting of draft prices, salary structures in the Minor Leagues, and other controls not applicable in other business endeavors. Baseball, it was concluded, was not a business but a sport.

From 1922 to near the middle of the twentieth century, the courts, astonishingly, stayed pretty clear of baseball operations. (Indeed, it is an interesting fact that to this day, well into the twenty-first century, and even with the enhanced rights of players, Organized Baseball's antitrust exemption remains in effect.) Although the Independent Carolina Baseball League of 1936–38 signed a great many Major and Minor League players without hesitation, and Organized Baseball clubs threatened to sue the Independent Carolina teams, no challenge of baseball's reserve clause made it through the federal courts to the Supreme Court. It was not until the late 1940s and the lawsuit filed by Danny Gardella that baseball, theretofore seemingly immune from antitrust litigation, experienced much reason for concern.

Gardella was an outfielder with the New York Giants during the war years of 1944 and 1945, a left-handed hitter and thrower, a stocky young man of twenty-four in 1944 and one of the first players ever to lift weights. He was an average player for that era. (Because of a perforated eardrum, he was declared 4-F.) In 1945 Gardella hit .272 with eighteen home runs. Dissatisfied with his salary offer from the Giants for 1946, he jumped to the newly formed, independent Mexican League, which had begun signing American players from both the Major and the Minor Leagues—twenty-three of them altogether—for in some cases double what they were making in the United States. New baseball commissioner A. B. "Happy" Chandler, who had succeeded Kenesaw Mountain Landis, immediately took action to blacklist any players who jumped their U.S. contracts, thereby prohibiting their return to Organized Baseball for five years and disallowing any U.S. team in Organized Baseball from playing against any semipro or amateur team, even in an exhibition game, if the semipro or amateur team used a player who had jumped and returned to the United States. Gardella, who played the 1946 season for the Veracruz Blues and hit .275 with thirteen home runs, decided after that season to return to the United States. Because he could not, under Chandler's ruling, resume play in Organized Baseball, he signed on with a semipro team for 1947. Frederick Johnson, a young Harvard-trained attorney and baseball fan, approached Gardella in 1947 about filing a lawsuit against Organized Baseball—for a contingency fee to be split fifty-fifty. Johnson had long believed that the reserve clause would not hold up in court.

In July 1948 Judge Henry Goddard of the U.S. Federal Court in the Southern District of New York held that his court had no jurisdiction in the case. But in a most significant observation, he noted that because of baseball's increased fees from broadcasting, both radio and most recently television, the 1922 court ruling might be subject to reversal. Johnson then took his case, using Goddard's comment as encouragement, to the Second Circuit Court of Appeals. Two of the justices on that court, which remanded the case to a lower court for a jury trial, held that given the amount of interstate broadcasting, baseball might indeed be subject to the antitrust laws. Scared to death about what might happen in the courts, Commissioner Chandler, with the backing of the owners, agreed to settle the Gardella case for $60,000—$30,000 of which went to Gardella.[12]

Two approaches to checking baseball's monopoly then went forward, one in Congress, the other in the courts. In July 1951 the Subcommittee on Monopoly Power of the House Judiciary Committee, under the chairmanship of Emmanuel Celler of Brooklyn, began hearings on the legality or illegality of baseball's activities. Celler was not above "prosecuting the owners," if they were in violation of the law—either that or it might be necessary to change the law. But the report of the committee in May 1952, which expressed greater interest in seeing baseball expand to more cities, did nothing to change things. Most of the witnesses, including players, urged retention of the reserve clause as essential to baseball's survival. On the other hand, committee members concluded that the sport should not have "blanket immunity" from antitrust laws. At this point Congress, in order to proceed, needed direction from a Supreme Court decision.[13]

It got clarification, of a sort, in the Toolson case of 1953. Following the Gardella settlement, several Minor League players with grievances against Organized Baseball went to court, the most notable among them Walter Kowalski and George Toolson. In the late 1940s the Brooklyn Dodgers had the largest Minor League system of all Major League clubs; they owned or had working agreements with twenty-four different teams, ranging from several in Class D to Triple-A. They controlled nearly five hundred players. Kowalski, an infielder who had played during the 1946 season with Lockport, New York, an unaffiliated team in the Class D Pony League, had his contract purchased by the Dodgers. In 1947 he again played Class D, this time in the North Atlantic League with Kingston, New York, where he had an excellent year. As the team's third baseman, he hit .318 with twenty-four triples and eleven home runs. Following that season the Dodgers assigned him to Pueblo of the Class A Western League. The purpose in jumping him over Classes C and B all the way to A was to protect him from the draft by another club, and not because the Dodgers expected him to play at Pueblo. Given the rule at the time, Class A players were subject to an unrestricted draft at a set price only if they had three years of professional experience; Kowalski had only two. This was but one move made by the Dodgers to control this young man's career—all in the interest of the Dodgers rather than his own. He eventually contacted a lawyer and filed suit against the Brooklyn team and Organized Baseball. The baseball man who had "protected" Kowalski: general manager of the Dodgers, Branch Rickey.

There are two ways to look at this case in light of the Continental League experience. One is that Rickey had about as much standing to challenge Organized Baseball as

British prime minister Winston Churchill had in attacking another country's right to possess colonies. Another is to see Rickey as not unlike President Franklin D. Roosevelt's choice of Joseph Kennedy to head the Securities Exchange Commission: he knew all the tricks, Roosevelt said, in defending the appointment.

When the Kowalski case and two others finally found their way to the U.S. Supreme Court, all three were subsumed under the name "Toolson." George Toolson was a big, right-handed pitcher, six feet one and 205 pounds, who had originally signed with the Boston Red Sox and had had several successful years in the high Minor Leagues, in 1946–48 with Louisville in the American Association and in 1949 with Newark of the International League. His best year was 1947 at Louisville, where he went 11-6 with a 3.19 earned run average. While at Newark in 1949, he was the "property" of the New York Yankees. Following the 1949 season, during which he went 5 and 5 and after Newark dropped out of the International League, the Yankees sent Toolson to Binghamton of the Class A Eastern League, a two-classification demotion. Toolson refused to report to Binghamton and instead signed to play the 1950 season with the San Francisco Seals of the Pacific Coast League. He appeared in three games for San Francisco in 1950, but because he had refused the assignment to the Eastern League, the Yankees, under Organized Baseball's rules, placed him on the ineligible list. He was thus blacklisted by baseball. He then filed an antitrust suit against the Yankees and Organized Baseball in the Federal District Court in Northern California. His case, legitimately when applied to any other American enterprise, was that he was being denied the right to make a living in the field of his choice, unless he played for a Yankees affiliate.

If Toolson and his attorneys thought the Supreme Court would overturn the Federal Baseball Ruling of 1922, they were badly mistaken. In a per curiam ruling, issued in 1953, a majority of the justices (seven of nine) held that the decision of 1922 would remain operative until Congress chose to pass legislation placing Organized Baseball under the jurisdiction of the Clayton and Sherman acts. Curiously, the justices said that they found no evidence that Congress in passing the Sherman and Clayton acts had any intention of bringing Organized Baseball under antitrust jurisdiction. Nor it would seem did Congress mention such an intention for a great many other enterprises. How many other cartels went unmentioned in 1890 and 1914? At any rate, Justice Holmes in 1922 never raised that issue; he and his fellow justices said baseball was not commerce.

Why did the court rule as it did? One reason was that Organized Baseball had developed for thirty years with an exemption from antitrust law; to change its status suddenly could damage the sport irreparably. The other reason, mentioned in the brief, was that totally free competition, while desirable in most areas of endeavor, could be highly detrimental if applied to baseball. There had to be some restrictions and rules to prevent players from moving about willynilly. In sum the Supreme Court thus said in 1953 that the decision of 1922 remained operative, unless Congress in the future chose to remove baseball's antitrust exemption. If the Supreme Court had erred in 1922, it was the prerogative of Congress to correct the error.[14]

But the court was not consistent when ruling on other cases. It ruled in 1955 on a theatrical case and on a boxing case that the activities of the theater and boxing were subject to the Sherman and Clayton acts. In 1957, in a professional football case, the court ruled that football was also subject to antitrust laws. But when it came to baseball, the justices held that it was the responsibility of Congress to change baseball's anomalous status. Congress tried but not very hard. A few of its members tried to address baseball's monopoly practices but were blocked in their efforts. Representative Emmanuel Celler, a tall, balding man of seventy-one years, from Brooklyn, who by 1957 showed his age after thirty-five years in Congress, was Organized Baseball's worst nightmare; he had, as noted, gone after the game in his hearings of 1951 and 1952. Incensed at the Dodgers proposed and then actual move to Los Angeles, he drafted legislation designed to limit baseball's antitrust exemption. When it became apparent that he could not get enough votes for a strongly restrictive bill, he watered it down. The bill he actually introduced allowed for exemption of all major professional sports if owners could prove that such exemptions were "reasonably necessary." This language, to any objective viewer, should have been benign enough for the owners. It was not. Representative Kenneth Keating from upstate New York, the polar opposite of Celler in many ways and certainly in the eyes of the baseball owners, was running for the U.S. Senate in 1958 (an office he attained) with the backing of Dan Topping, owner of the Yankees, and other members of the baseball establishment. He introduced legislation in the House, competing with Celler's bill, that would have granted exemption from the antitrust laws to all major sports—a bill that might have been a legal travesty but had the backing of nearly half the House and the Senate. Keating's bill, needless to say, had the enthusiastic support of all the Major League Baseball owners.[15]

Keating's bill might have passed had it not been for Senator Estes Kefauver of Tennessee and the bumbling, ill-prepared ramblings of the Washington Senators' owner,

Calvin Griffith. Kefauver had a reelection campaign coming up in 1960; that and his all-consuming ego, which forced him always to remain in the spotlight, also led to his promotion of the fact that he favored equality of opportunity in the old progressive sense. As chair of the Senate Judiciary Subcommittee on Antitrust and Monopoly in the summer of 1958, he held hearings on the Keating bill. He had serious doubts about the passage of a blanket exemption. Because Griffith had issued a public pronouncement about taking the Senators to Minneapolis, he was invited to address the committee, along with a bevy of baseball stars, executives, and the inimitable Casey Stengel. Griffith's announcement about leaving Washington and his corollary comments about baseball being a business rather than a sport—a notion then contrary to the position of the game's leaders—led Kefauver's committee to table the legislation as too sweeping, too broad. So Celler's efforts had come to nothing; Keating's efforts fortunately had come to nothing; Kefauver's efforts had come to nothing. By the end of 1958, nothing to regulate baseball had passed Congress.

But there was still hope. There were three possibilities for legislation: exempt all professional sports from antitrust action; subject all sports to equal treatment as business engaged in interstate commerce and hence under the authority of antitrust law (football owners complained bitterly about baseball's special status); or craft some compromise of the two positions that would provide limited immunity. In February 1959 Kefauver introduced legislation exempting all professional teams from many of the provisions of the antitrust laws, but not exempting baseball teams that controlled or reserved more than eighty players at a time. Eventually the bill reduced the number to be controlled to

THE HORSEHIDE CARTEL CHALLENGED

only forty, a measure that would have been of inestimable help to the Continental League had it passed.[16]

Rickey endorsed the forty-player limit in the fall of 1959, in the hope that Major League executives would come to their senses. But he did so simultaneously with reaching the conclusion that the Continental League would probably have to go independent. At the winter meetings in Miami in December, he listened, as noted previously, to a great deal of blather about internal expansion—not in 1960 but in 1961. Rickey called the various Continental League owners together for a meeting at the Fontanblieu Hotel. His purpose was to seek their agreement to take the existing Major League owners to court; all the third-league owners would become plaintiffs in the case. The owners did not give him that permission. But Bill Shea and Rickey himself began a private and public drumbeat that surely discomfited the owners of the National and the American Leagues. They talked about legal action and "outlaw status."

By the end of the 1950s, baseball executives were telling Rickey privately that the reserve clause, despite their many efforts to preserve it, was a moribund concept, an artifact of an earlier era in the game's development. "The attorneys for the Commissioner and the Leagues," Rickey noted in November 1959, "are not hesitant to say that the reserve clause in players' contracts will no longer hold up."[17] These same individuals had been saying for several years that another case could not be taken to the Supreme Court—which is precisely what Rickey had in mind doing at the end of 1959. An interesting conundrum had thus emerged: the Supreme Court had said that the anomalous position of baseball under the antitrust laws should be corrected in Congress. Congress had moved tepidly in the 1950s because it thought it must follow the courts. Baseball officials knew that the reserve clause would not hold up but worked very hard indeed to preserve it. It was against this backdrop—and Rickey's and Shea's comments about going independent—that Senator Kefauver in 1960 proposed legislation to assist the Continental League.

Which parts of Organized Baseball's monopoly should be considered the most insidious is an open question. The reserve clause in the standard players' contract stated: "Each year, on or before March 1st (or if Sunday then the succeeding business day) next following the playing season covered by this contract, by written notice to the Player, the Club or any assignee thereof, may renew this contract for the term of that year except that the salary rate shall be such as the parties may then agree upon." Pending an appeal to the commissioner's office or the head of the National Association, the contract stated further, "the Player will accept the salary as fixed by the club or else will not play otherwise than for the club or for an assignee thereof."[18] (The latter means another team to which the player might be traded or assigned.) The understanding was that with only the slightest restriction the club initially signing a player could control him for as long as he played the game. The club could fine him, suspend him, blacklist him, trade him, sell him, and completely control his professional life.

Through a good part of the twentieth century, the reserve system often extended to a second degree. If an independent club or one operating semi-independently signed a player to a standard contract and then concluded a working agreement through which it took operating funds from another, higher-level club, the latter usually gained first rights to the player who had signed with the former. For years this was the way the Pacific Coast League clubs functioned in relation to the National and the American Leagues. The

THE HORSEHIDE CARTEL CHALLENGED

reserve clause bound players in this manner at all levels of the Minor Leagues.

As the forgoing implies, the reserve clause as the primary vehicle of player exploitation has an inglorious history. In 1876 the National League brought some order to the world of professional baseball, which had existed in some form or other since 1869, when the Cincinnati Red Stockings began openly paying players. Prior to 1869 those who played baseball saw themselves participating in a gentleman's game, a pastime engaged in on weekends for exercise and recreation. But before long the game became a spectator sport as well as an exercise activity; people proved willing to pay to watch baseball. The National League capitalized on the interest with teams in eight cities: Chicago, Philadelphia, Boston, Hartford, New York, St. Louis, Cincinnati, and Louisville—all charging admission and paying players. Although the league brought some semblance of an ordered, rational professional system, players frequently jumped from team to team in midseason, causing serious disruption in pennant races.

In the off-season of 1878–79, National League team owners made an agreement not to hire players from other ball clubs during the season; and because that seemed to make sense in an era hostile to labor, they followed up that same winter with a system allowing each team to protect or reserve five players each year, who would remain unavailable to other teams. This was the beginning of the reserve clause. In 1883 owners decided that reserving players worked so well—worked to keep good players from raids by other clubs but also to keep salaries in check—that they would extend the reserve system to the entire roster. By 1887 and further in the 1890s, the clause became a part of the standard players' contract.

Early on, players considered it an honor to be reserved. But they soon learned that they had lost their negotiating power and frequently found themselves in less than desirable playing situations, with either noncompetitive teams or those with abusive management. Minor League clubs hoped to reserve their players as well, but National League owners refused, it is interesting to note, to recognize their reserve contracts with players. Until a draft system could be worked out and some payment made for players, owners of Minor League clubs operated at a serious disadvantage because they lost their best players to the Major League, seemingly without recourse. By the twentieth century, however, Minor League clubs were utilizing a reserve system nearly as restrictive to players as that at the Major League level.

Over the years there were several challenges to the reserve system. In the early twentieth century a threat came from the American League, in 1901–3, during which time the new league signed players from both Minor and Major League rosters. In 1903, however, the owners of both leagues resolved the threat with a new National Agreement embracing the reserve clause and the Minor League draft. As yet, and until 1965, there was no draft of amateur players. For over sixty years amateurs were the only baseball players who had negotiating power, a condition owners always lamented. In the post–World War II era as bonuses escalated in value, owners tried a variety of tactics to limit such payments. They finally succeeded in 1965 with the amateur draft, a procedure of questionable legality, in effect to this day.

Another challenge to the system came with the Federal League of 1914–15 and its teams' signing of players under contract to National and American League clubs. After two years the Federals went out of business, the end coming in a negotiated settlement with the more established leagues. A third challenge come from the Mexican League after World War II, but that challenge played itself out quickly owing to financial problems within that circuit.

After 1890, with the passage of the Sherman Antitrust Act and in 1914 with its extension in the Clayton Act, the most worrisome concern for the owners was the possibility of court action declaring baseball a monopoly with its executives subject to penalty under federal law. A declaration that labor conditions in baseball constituted a monopsony was always a distinct possibility; that is to say, that Organized Baseball had created an artificial market situation in which the seller of labor was limited to one buyer. That worry was allayed with the Supreme Court ruling of 1922.

Owners' questionable treatment even of star players, deriving in the main from the reserve clause, remained palpable for many years. At the Major League level a couple of cases stand out. In 1937 Joe DiMaggio, the New York Yankees' key drawing card, received a salary of fifteen thousand dollars while leading the club to its second consecutive World Series championship. DiMaggio hit .346 while leading the league in home runs with 46, runs scored with 151, and had 167 RBIs. In the winter of 1938 Jacob Ruppert, the Yankees' owner, offered the young star exactly the same salary for the 1938 season, then eventually raised his offer to twenty-five thousand dollars. This was not chicken feed during the Great Depression, but it did not approximate the forty-six thousand dollars that DiMaggio thought he was worth. (Worth is extremely hard to determine, but DiMaggio, considering gate attendance alone, was probably worth much more than the forty-six thousand dollars he demanded.) His only recourse was to hold out. Ruppert refused to budge. He refused to allow his young star to come to spring training unless DiMaggio signed. Then Ruppert issued inflammatory press releases from Florida about the ungrateful young Yankee demanding an exorbitant salary when times were so tough for all Americans.

When the season started with Myril Hoag in center-field, DiMaggio caved in and signed on Ruppert's terms. Ruppert then proceeded to dock DiMaggio's pay until he got in playing shape, and he insisted that the player pay his own expenses on road trips. Altogether he deducted about two thousand dollars from DiMaggio's new salary. Yankees fans, impressed by merciless stories owing to the usual cozy relationship between owners and the press, booed DiMaggio for much of the 1938 season, a year in which he hit .324 with 32 home runs and drove in 140, while striking out only 21 times in 599 official at bats—and again led the team to the pennant and a World Series victory.

In 1952 Ralph Kiner, the Pittsburgh Pirates star left fielder and home run hitter, the only real Major League star on what was a truly sorry ball club, hit thirty-seven home runs to lead the league for the seventh straight season, his first seven seasons in the Major Leagues. No one had ever done that before, or has since. But Branch Rickey, then the Pirates general manager, did not like Kiner. Kiner did not have a strong throwing arm, nor was he fleet afoot. He was the team's player representative, and soon to be the league's representative, active in the growing players' rights movement, activity anathema to Rickey. Rickey frequently denigrated Kiner's accomplishments with comments that he hit all those home runs because of Greenberg Gardens, the bullpen arrangement in left field that brought the fence in to help Hank Greenberg, acquired from the Detroit Tigers in 1947, hit more home runs. It worked for Greenberg in 1947, but Kiner benefitted most, and after Greenberg's retirement following that one season, the shortened fence came to be known as Kiner's Corner. But in spacious Forbes Field, where the Pirates played, Kiner's Corner was not all that inviting to a power hitter. It was still 335 feet down the left-field line, and it took a big poke to hit the ball out in left center, and in center field. All that aside, most important to Rickey, Kiner was making a salary of ninety thousand dollars.

The Pirates finished an abysmal last in 1952 and despite having Kiner as the main drawing card, dropped three hundred thousand in attendance. For 1953 Rickey offered Kiner a contract calling for a 22.5 percent cut; he was not impressed with his star's slugging performance. "We finished last with you. We can finish last without you," Rickey said. Kiner, after a lengthy holdout, took a fifteen-thousand-dollar cut. On June 4, 1953, Rickey traded him to the Chicago Cubs in a ten-player deal that netted the Pirates very little player talent but one hundred thousand dollars in cash. Kiner ended that season with 35 home runs, 116 RBIs, over 100 walks for the sixth straight season, and a batting average of .279.

Major League clubs' treatment of young, newly signed players was often more shameful than its handling of established stars. In the 1950s, when owners routinely colluded to keep bonuses low, they concluded an agreement stipulating that if a ball club gave a player more than four thousand dollars in bonus money, that player had to be placed on the Major League club's twenty-five-man roster immediately. This meant that the player could not acquire Minor League seasoning or development and had to sit in the Major League dugout. Assuming the signee was not ready to play in the big leagues, the ball club granting the bonus was effectively limited to a twenty-four-man roster. It meant further that few teams handed out bonuses of over four thousand dollars; the rule had the desired effect as a disincentive to granting bonuses—or players accepting them.

A common practice during the 1950s, one followed with numerous friends of mine and one I was warned to avoid, was to give a player a contingency bonus. A Major League club would sign a player to a contract calling for, say, a three-thousand-dollar bonus if he were still with the Minor League club to which he had been assigned, after thirty days. On the twenty-ninth day the club would release the player. If the player had not done especially well, had not gotten off to a good start, he would be on his own, usually to go home and find another line of work or sign with another Major League team. If he was a standout prospect but one who had gotten off to a slow start, the club on the thirty-first day would offer to sign him again, without a bonus. Rather than start over, or try to do so with a new ball club, the player, more often than not, would re-sign.

At the Minor League level owners' exploitation of players—those they had signed and owned outright—was often even more disgraceful. Because clubs could fine players with almost no recourse for the player, fines became a common way of taking away bonus money. In a famous instance, in the North Carolina State League a player, a pitcher, whose name I cannot recall, had a clause in his contract calling for a modest one-hundred-dollar bonus if he won fifteen games. On the date of his fifteenth win, the first game of a doubleheader, the manager of the ball club congratulated him on his performance, then told him he could shower and sit in the stands for the second game—unusual generosity for Class D baseball, where clubs carried only fifteen players and all bodies were needed, if for no other reason than to coach first base. The team owner then fined the young man one hundred dollars for being out of uniform for that game—a setup arrangement with the manager.

Minor and Major League clubs paid inadequate attention to injuries to Minor League players as well. A concussion meant almost nothing. As long as a player could still identify what city he was in, or come close, he stayed in the game. If one had an injury that might take extended time to heal, he had to play anyway. If he could not play effectively, he was released. I experienced this firsthand in 1957. A serious groin injury that limited my ability to swing the bat, that cut down on the fluidity of my swing and interfered with my running speed, led Andy Gilbert, my manager at Muskogee, to recommend my release by the Giants.

All of us who thought about such things hoped that the Continental League would bring change. The Supreme Court in 1922 had exempted baseball from the antitrust laws, but did, or could, the court exempt Organized Baseball from provisions of the Thirteenth and the Fourteenth Amendments of the U.S. Constitution. Frederick Johnson in the Gardella case saw the reserve system as a violation of antitrust law and the Fourteenth Amendment. When Curt Flood, the star St. Louis Cardinal outfielder, refused his trade from St. Louis to Philadelphia and challenged the reserve clause in court in the early 1970s, Arthur Goldberg, former associate justice of the Supreme Court and Flood's attorney, argued that the clause violated not only the antitrust laws but also the Thirteenth Amendment. Rickey was a lawyer as well as a baseball man. As he contemplated a court case against baseball at the end of 1959, he kept all these things in mind.

If the reserve clause ranks first in insidiousness, territorial rights rank a close second. "So long as the Major Leagues are able to maintain their absolute monopoly on players and territories," Rickey told a group of reporters in Miami, "we will find ourselves unable to complete the formation of the Continental League."[19] Access to Minor League territory became a major issue in early 1960—an issue that was both complicated and simple: complicated because under its exemption from the antitrust laws, Organized Baseball could establish rules keeping competition out of any given club's area in either the Major or the Minor Leagues; simple because in logic and in accord with American principles of fair play, any aspiring entrepreneur could open a business wherever he or she wished. Rand Dixon, Senator Kefauver's assistant, put it well when he asked rhetorically why a Continental League club should have to pay a fee or purchase access if it wished to locate a franchise in Minor League territory. Would the owner of a grocery store have to pay a fee to another store already operating on a given street before opening a store on that same street? The answer, in most circumstances, was a patently obvious no. Were the Continental League to operate independently, which is what Dixon recommended and Kefauver favored as well, it could locate clubs wherever it wished, paying no fee. But Dixon in his grocery store analogy was confusing the American ideal with the reality of baseball's monopoly.[20]

As long as Rickey, Shea, and the owners in the third league sought to operate within the rules of Organized Baseball, arbitrary as those rules could be, they were forced to negotiate for access to cities in which they planned franchises. Minor League owners in those cities sought to extract, not surprisingly, exorbitant payments. President of the International League Frank "Shag" Shaughnessy, Rickey's friend and associate for over thirty years, demanded $1,000,000 for the rights to Toronto, a longtime Triple-A city, and a similar $1,000,000 fee for the right to place a team in Buffalo.

1. Reynoldsville (Pennsylvania) Little League
Dodgers, 1950. Russ Buhite is in the back row,
second from left. (Courtesy of the author)

2. *(Opposite top)* Russ Buhite with the Hastings (Nebraska) Giants, Nebraska State League, 1957. (Courtesy of the author)

3. *(Opposite bottom)* Russ Buhite, spring training 1958 at Thomasville, Georgia, in the Baltimore Orioles organization. (Courtesy of the author)

4. *(Above)* Rutherford County Owls, 1960. *Rear, left to right*: Ray Searcy, p; Troy Searcy, of; Gary Cowan, c; Richard Stauffer, p; George Ferrell, of; Gene Garnell, p; Jim Flowers, p. *Front, left to right*: batboy; Willie MacDonald, 2b; Enrique Bonitto, ss; Charles Harris, 3b; Joe Priestes, of; Tommy Jamieson, p. *Not pictured*: Russ Buhite, 1b, of; Leonard Jackson, c, inf, manager; Tommy McIntyre, p. (Courtesy of George Ferrell)

5. Rutherford County Owls, 1960. Based in Forest City, North Carolina. *Left to right*: Enrique Bonitto, Willie MacDonald, Russ Buhite, Ray Searcy, Jim Flowers. (Courtesy of the author)

6. George Ferrell with the Rutherford County Owls, 1960. (Courtesy of George Ferrell)

7. Jim Poole with the Philadelphia Athletics, 1925–27. (National Baseball Hall of Fame Library, Cooperstown, New York)

8. Jim Poole as manager and player with Fort Pierce, Florida, East Coast League, 1941. With him are his two sons, Jim Jr. (*left*) and Phil (*right*), who also played on the team. (National Baseball Hall of Fame Library, Cooperstown, New York)

9. John Moss, 2007. (Courtesy of the Kings Mountain Historical Museum)

10. Bruce Greene, owner of the Rutherford County Owls, 1960. Based in Forest City, North Carolina. (Courtesy of Beth Greene Wheeler)

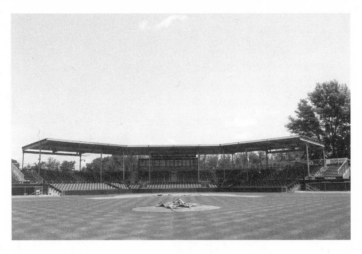

11. The Forest City ballpark as it appears now. (Courtesy of Beth Greene Wheeler)

12. Gastonia Legion Field as it looks now and in 1960. (Courtesy of Matthew Grant and Gary Humphries)

"I cannot face my God much longer knowing that His black creatures are held separate and distinct from His white creatures in the game that has given me all that I can call my own."

Dodger boss Rickey realized a lifelong ambition when he broke baseball's color line by signing Jackie Robinson (below). Behind Rickey is a picture of Abe Lincoln.

A Branch Grows in Brooklyn

Jackie Robinson

Branch Rickey flourishes in Flatbush, champions the Negro in baseball, and is the father of major league's profitable farm system

By TIM COHANE

Wesley Branch Rickey, 64-year-old president of the Brooklyn Dodgers, enjoys an indifferent press. Some sportswriters roar regularly for his head to be brought in on home plate, preferably with a baseball in his mouth as a gag in the literal sense. Others are less bloodthirsty.

"Branch has so got into the habit of quoting scripture," these latter point out, "that even when his mo- tives are purely altruistic, his critics are still dubious."

Most Tongmen and Pollyannas alike, however, hailed Rickey in print or in private when he brought the Negro into modern organized baseball for the first time recently by signing Jackie Robinson, a shortstop, to a contract with the Dodgers' farm team at Montreal.

Nobody could reasonably suspect materialistic mo- tives. Negro stars are not imperative to the pennant Rickey labors toward, nor could they improve attendance at Eb- bets Field where a third-place team played to over a mil- lion paying fans last season.

In fact, signing Robinson may cost Rickey money, and Branch is about as allergic to money as he is to Rickey. Already, talent bird dogs have routed young prospects away from Brooklyn, because **(Continued on page 72)**

13. Branch Rickey. (Photo by Harold Rhodenbaugh, from Tim Cohane, "A Branch Grows in Brooklyn," *Look*, March 19, 1946, 70, *Look* Magazine Photograph Collection, Prints and Photographs Division, Library of Congress LC-USZ62-119888)

14. William Shea, major promoter of the Continental League. (National Baseball Hall of Fame Library, Cooperstown, New York)

15. Leaders of Houston's CL efforts, George Kirksey (*left*) and Craig Cullinan (*right*). (George Kirksey Papers, courtesy of Special Collections, University of Houston Libraries)

16. Senator Estes Kefauver,
undated photograph.
(U.S. Senate Historical Office)

17. Ford Frick, commissioner of baseball.
(National Baseball Hall of Fame Library,
Cooperstown, New York)

18. *Left to right*: Warren Giles, president of the National League; Ford Frick, commissioner of baseball; Joe Cronin, president of the American League. (National Baseball Hall of Fame Library, Cooperstown, New York)

19. Walter O'Malley, owner of the Los Angeles Dodgers. (National Baseball Hall of Fame Library, Cooperstown, New York)

Edward Doherty, president of the American Association, wanted $850,000 for Minneapolis-St. Paul. The ridiculousness of these fees, not to say the right to seek a fee, became clear to Rickey when Walter O'Malley offered to sell the Montreal club to the Continental League (Montreal was not one of the cities proposed for the new league and would not become one unless another city dropped out) for a price of $150,000, which included twelve players. Rickey also quickly pointed out that when the Dodgers and the Giants moved to Los Angeles and San Francisco respectively, they paid a total of only $850,000 for access to both cities.

Houston provided a further example of the absurdity of it all. Following the 1959 season, the St. Louis Cardinals offered their class Double-A Texas League affiliate, which had lost money during the 1958 season and did not operate in 1959, for sale for $100,000. When the Continental League sought to locate a club in Houston, Marty Marion, the old Cardinal shortstop and then president of the Houston Buffs, insisted, at the instance of the Cardinals, that the club receive payment of $495,000 for rights to the territory. That the fees sought were clearly arbitrary there is little doubt, but something else was going on as well: Organized Baseball was attempting to block the Continental League.

At one point in the territorial negotiations, Rickey proposed what he thought was a fair solution: he suggested arbitration as a way of determining prices. Ford Frick seemed to agree but then backed away from the idea, because his bosses, the owners, told him to do so. Rickey then suggested a formula based on the one used when the St. Louis Browns moved to Baltimore: 7 cents per paying customer for three years, based on the previous three years' paid attendance (a total of $48,000). For Buffalo, based on its gate for the 1958, 1959, and 1960 seasons, using the Baltimore formula, the fee would have been $76,000. The fee paid to Toronto would have been similar. Frick would not accept this solution or any other, no matter how equitable. Territorial monopoly, like the reserve clause, could be used as a blocking device. To this end, in the spring of 1960 Organized Baseball began asking $850,000 for each Minor League territory.[21] As noted earlier the Yankees were the most aggrieved because although they claimed exclusive rights to New York City, the commissioner had said that the territory was open to a another club. If the Continental League located there, and it was essential to the league's viability that it do so, it would owe no indemnity to the Yankees. The Yankees were determined to stop the new league.

Continental League owners and backers, and of course Rickey himself, remained hopeful during the early months of 1960. Dallas now seemed firm as a franchise, after some apparent misgivings. The Twin Cities no longer saw much chance of getting the Washington Senators. Hence the Minneapolis franchise seemed set as well. Buffalo came on board officially on January 29 as the eighth city. The new league existed in full, at least on paper. Beyond all that, Senator Kefauver was preparing to help the new league with legislation. Rickey proposed, and all the owners agreed, that if any of the clubs defected to the National or the American League, they would owe the third league $2.5 million in reparations, a serious bar to defection. If there was a defector, Montreal would be added in its place.[22]

As part of the flurry of optimism, Rickey assured all the owners in the new league that no one would lose money. The reasons? For one thing the new league would be balanced in talent. In 1960 each existing Major League club employed about a dozen full-time scouts to identify and sign free-agent players. All the National and American League clubs also used what were called "bird dog" scouts, who were paid on a commission basis when they found players for the Major League organization. Thus the total number of scouts working for a Major League team at any given time was about thirty, at a cost of between $100,000 and $300,000 per year. Rickey proposed hiring a total of five or six men who would scout for the whole Continental League. These scouts could easily obtain information on four hundred players per year. The league's clubs would then have the right to choose from this pool of players, by lot, according to perceived need and negotiate with and presumably sign their choices. This approach would be inexpensive and would, Rickey believed, create far more equity among teams than that in either the National or the American League. No club would find itself out of the pennant race by midsummer, or in any event would not in normal circumstances and barring injuries find itself in that position. Also, to bring further equity visiting clubs, because they created a significant part of the entertainment value, would receive forty cents per capita from the home club's gate receipts for every game; and the league would sign a television deal and pool two-thirds of all the TV revenue. The Continental League would provide serious, high-quality baseball competition as teams in the league played one another—and in short order, would be prepared to compete with other Major League clubs in the World Series.[23]

Rickey also knew how much it would cost to field a team. Combined pay for players, the manager, and a trainer would amount to roughly $295,000. Never known as one to overpay his players, Rickey must have calculated this figure using the then-minimum salary of $7,000. If $295,000 is divided twenty-seven ways evenly, the salary for twenty-five players, a manager, and a trainer would have been $10,025 each. If two coaches were included, the amount for each, divided evenly, would have been $10,172. Rickey would have, with some exceptions, paid the manager more than the players and the coaches a bit less; hence he had in mind something close to the players' minimum. Social security would cost $25,000. Regular-season team travel would run $50,000. Hotel and meals would be $25,000. Two sets of uniforms, home and away, would cost $5,000, or roughly $100 per uniform per player—$200 each for twenty-five players, not counting the coaches and the manager. Bats and other equipment would run $2,500. Training equipment would cost $7,500. Spring training expenses would be about $40,000. Park help would be $75,000. Player procurement, a farm director, and support for Minor League clubs would come to $350,000. Though these figures, even adjusted to present-day dollars, seem ridiculously low, they were pretty realistic for the time, assuming incidental expenses were thrown in. So not only would ball clubs in the Continental League not lose money by virtue of low attendance, or a failure to share in television revenue, or any other unfair practices; they would have manageable costs. The wealthy new owners would have no difficulty in fielding teams.[24]

But despite the optimism, there were problems apparent in early 1960. When Rickey met with Ford Frick on February 2, the commissioner stressed financial issues: the cost of organizing and getting started and the costs of the pension plan for players. The biggest obstacle, however, according to Frick, was compensating Minor League owners for invading their territories and satisfying the demands of Major League owners who were heavily invested in many of these Minor League cities. All these costs, if the Continental League wanted acceptance into Organized Baseball, would have to be addressed. More than that, Frick hinted, the new league would have to overcome the objection of the Yankees to a team in New York. "You've got a tough job," Frick told Rickey. "I don't know whether you can do it or not." Rickey's reply: "Don't try to scare me."[25]

Rickey and the Continental League owners were counting on Senator Kefauver for help. Kefauver introduced a bill in the Senate Judiciary Committee in May, one that had been several months in the making, that constituted general sports antitrust legislation. It exempted basketball, football, and hockey from provisions of the Sherman and Clayton acts, thereby satisfying executives in those sports. The legislation set a limit on the number of players subject to baseball's reserve clause: a team could sign 100 players and make them subject to reserve, but after four years at least 60 of those players had to be made available for other clubs to draft. In other words, a Major League club could maintain full control forever of 40 players plus 60 more for their first four years in Organized Baseball; all others would be available for an unrestricted draft. In the short run, because the Continental League clubs would need established or experienced players to join the young, inexperienced players they signed, and each National and American League club "owned" between 250 and 400 players, this legislation would have provided a windfall. If Rickey, as the inventor of the farm system that controlled hundreds of players, worried that this provision of Kefauver's legislation made him look terribly hypocritical, he kept it to himself. He saw the bill as a lifeline for the new league. Needless to say, in view of the squabbling over territory and indemnities, he also favored the restriction Kefauver's legislation placed on territorial control; it set a thirty-five-mile limit.

In May 1960, executives of the new league and the baseball establishment trundled off to Washington to testify before Kefauver's committee. The arguments of the establishment, the lords of baseball, were direct, indeed brazen. Ford Frick's views had been well known since the 1950s: antitrust laws, the commissioner said, were designed to regulate big business, and baseball was not big business. In 1950 aggregate income for all the Major and Minor Leagues was only $65,000,000. In 1956 it was less: only $60,000,000. Only four Major League teams made money on a consistent basis through the 1950s. Many teams lost money. At the beginning of the 1960s, baseball was simply not a significant economic enterprise. (Though it must be pointed out that it was far more profitable than either professional football or boxing.) Frick made a strong argument for retaining the reserve clause in its totality, always the most critical antitrust issue. No one in Congress, interestingly enough, chose to challenge the owners on the basis of the Thirteenth Amendment.

"The reserve clause," the commissioner intoned, "is not merely a provision in a player's contract, but also incorporates a reticulated system of rules and regulations which enable, indeed require, the entire baseball organization to respect and enforce each club's exclusive and continuous right to the service of its players." Even a five-year reserve clause, a possible compromise suggested at one point, or a numerical limit on reserved players, Frick testified, "would be detrimental to baseball—to the game's integrity, to the player's development, and to the club's ability to plan and maintain a competitive team." If baseball came under the antitrust laws, its leader claimed, one player after another with "failures" or "gripes" would go to the courts seeking treble damages. As to Kefauver's legislation, he said it was "pernicious and vicious" and "dangerous" for baseball.[26]

Although Rickey was not in favor of criminal penalties for baseball executives who disregarded the strictures of

Kefauver's legislation, a provision of the bill that was eventually dropped, he testified strongly in favor of the overall measure. One of his arguments in favor of an annual draft was its presumed beneficial effect in cutting down on amateur bonuses. Such bonuses, he had long believed, had a baneful effect on a young, unproven player who might become lazy if given a large sum of money up front. Moreover, a player who received a large bonus could easily become morally corrupt and would almost always be the object of envy and jealousy of his teammates, especially his older, more experienced teammates. Once again, if the president of the Continental League saw any corruption in his own prior experience in selling players by the barrel full and personally taking 10 percent of the sale price, he did not betray the thought.

Frick had said repeatedly that elimination of the reserve clause or even any restriction on it would destroy the Minor Leagues. Rickey countered that the new league would create a multitude of jobs at both the Major and the Minor League level (320 at the Major League level alone, if numbered by the forty-man roster, and that was not counting managers and coaches). But in any case where did the current owners get the standing to make proclamations about saving the Minor Leagues? They had presided over the reduction of the Minor Leagues from fifty-nine in 1949 to just twenty-one in 1960. Rickey went on to say he had believed, or been led to believe, that baseball's executives wanted his league to succeed, but he was wrong in that judgment.[27]

Bill Shea was more blunt in his assessment than Rickey. He announced that if the Kefauver legislation failed, the Continental League would have an important decision: it could either fold up or go "outlaw." In February the New York Board of Estimates had approved, at the strongest possible urging of Robert Moses, the construction of the new stadium in Flushing Meadows. Shea would use that stadium; he would have his new league, even if a war were necessary to get it.

"Outlaw" was not a word that rang true with Rand Dixon of Kefauver's staff. He urged Rickey and his owners to proceed with the new league on the belief that the existing leagues were the "outlaws." In other words the Continental League should assume "that the reserve clause [was] illegal; that it was no longer in effect; that the major leagues were operating outside the law"; and that the Major Leagues could not risk another reserve clause case going to the Supreme Court. The new league should also stop trying to negotiate for territory; that made absolutely no sense, as the courts would no longer uphold the silly idea of territorial monopoly. Hence what Rickey and the Continental League owners should do was simply begin signing established Major League players. After the new league signed two or three of them, the Major League establishment would come to the new league "hat in hand."[28]

More and more Rickey was coming around to Dixon's point of view, though he was not there quite yet. He proposed to his third-league owners that instead of giving large bonuses they should agree among themselves to double the salaries of any established Major Leaguers they wished to sign. That would not have been an expensive proposition in an era in which the Major League minimum salary was seven thousand dollars. In the fall of 1959, as Calvin Griffith was making noises about a move to Minneapolis, Rickey talked semi-openly of signing Harmon Killebrew, then a young power hitter with the Senators and eventually a Hall of Fame quality player, to a Continental League contract—and he made sure Ford Frick knew of his proposal.[29]

The thoughts of Senator Kefauver, unlike those of his assistant Dixon, are not entirely clear. He hailed the idea of greater opportunity in baseball. He deplored monopoly practices and what they did to the American economy. He certainly wanted the Continental League to succeed, and he may have taken campaign contributions from Continental League owners, though there is no definitive proof, none in the Kefauver Papers, of his doing so. His consuming passion was calling attention to himself prior to the 1960 senatorial election in Tennessee, which promised to be hotly contested.

It should have become apparent to any knowledgeable observer that the bill to help the Continental League would find difficult sledding. Kefauver himself did not attend the hearings, as he had more important matters to attend to back in Tennessee.[30] After testifying Rickey spent much of his time in Pittsburgh with his ailing wife. Senator Keating from New York, who had for a brief time encouraged the Continental Leaguers but who was in the pocket of the existing leagues, began voicing opposition to any legislation that might, in his phrasing, do harm to Organized Baseball. The hearings ended without a favorable recommendation of the Kefauver bill; Keating was able to block the legislation at this stage.

The legislation, in June, became the vehicle for a vigorous political struggle between Senate majority leader Lyndon Johnson of Texas, who was battling John F. Kennedy for the presidential nomination, and the "generalissimo" of lobbyists, Paul Porter. Born in Joplin, Missouri, but raised in Kentucky, Porter, who earned a law degree at the University of Kentucky, had been an administrator in the Office of Price Administration during World War II and then became the chairman of the Federal Communications Commission. In 1946 he organized the Washington law firm in which Abe

Fortas became a partner—a firm that developed a reputation as one of Washington's most powerful. Porter became well known for his connections and for his skill as a political manipulator. He took up the case of Organized Baseball with enthusiastic aggressiveness, believing firmly that baseball could not take the blows proposed in the Kefauver legislation.

Confident in his connections with the Senate, Porter told the established owners that the Continental League had no chance of winning the legislative battle—and he was eventually proven correct. But prior to victory he came up against the most powerful man in Congress in Lyndon Johnson. George Kirksey and Craig Cullinan, the developers of the Houston franchise in the new league, had gotten to Johnson. Whether they greased Johnson's palms is unknown, but the majority leader suddenly became a great baseball fan and a supporter of the new league. He began encouraging support for the Kefauver bill, pressuring other senators to get behind the measure as a way to take baseball to more U.S. cities—as a way, Johnson hoped, to get a Major League team in Texas.

Johnson was powerful and smart. Porter was an outstanding lobbyist. In short order Porter reached out to Senator Philip Hart, a Democrat from Michigan, destined to become a major player himself in liberal causes. As a liberal he might have been expected to support limitation on corporate greed, but especially on the flouting of antitrust law. Unfortunately for the Continental League, Hart also happened to be the brother-in-law of Walter "Spike" Briggs, son of the longtime owner of the Detroit Tigers, Walter Owen Briggs. Young Briggs had himself served for a time as vice president and general manager of the club. The Tigers played in Briggs Stadium. Married to "Spike" Briggs's sister, Hart himself was a stockholder in the Tigers' franchise, a baseball enthusiast who, even without Porter's encouragement, would work hard to stop the Kefauver bill. He believed any limitation on the reserve system constituted a threat to the stability of baseball, a possible undermining of the high competitive quality of the nation's greatest sport. He found his financial interest reinforced by his sentimental interest—or the other way around.

By the end of June 1960, it had become apparent that the proposed Kefauver legislation would face serious opposition. Politicians were interested in baseball to be sure, but they were far more interested in preserving their seats, in gaining or retaining majority control in Congress, and, of course, in nominating candidates for the November election. Baseball was simply not the highest priority in Washington that summer. The major obstacle in the Senate came in the form of legislation introduced by Republican senator Alexander Wiley of Wisconsin, who knew what he was doing. His bill provided that all professional sports, football, basketball, and hockey, receive the same antitrust exemptions as baseball; all four sports would be combined in the exempt category. All would be able to reserve players, control their territories through strict rules, control their television revenues: control, control, control. And the proposed player draft would be abandoned. Wiley's bill, voted on in the full Senate, passed 45–41. This development represented an ominous portent for the Continental League. Through a legislative maneuver, the Kefauver bill was sent back to the Judiciary Committee for future consideration. Future consideration, given the Wiley amendment, meant almost certain defeat.[31]

The key feature of the Kefauver legislation was access to players. If the Major League teams could control roughly 4,200 players and gave the Continental League no way to sign any of them but the castoffs, how could the new league join the Major Leagues? Of course, it could not, which was exactly the intention of the existing owners. Rickey and the owners in the new league could still go independent, which was a live possibility in the spring of 1960. That would allow them to sign whomever they wished. They could emulate the new American Football League, which was doing just that, that is to say, rejecting the blandishments, the threats, the possible legal action from the National Football League and going on its own. One thing the Continental League did prepare to do, indeed had already started doing whether or not it received the imprimatur of Organized Baseball, was begin developing players.

The Houston Continental League club advanced a Minor League development plan early on. In October 1959 executives of that organization told Rickey they wanted three Minor League teams right away, meaning in 1960: one in Class Triple-A, one in Class C, and one at the Class D level. Donald V. Labbruzzo, the general manager of the Buffalo franchise in the International League, who was a major supporter of the new league idea, suggested that each Continental League club sponsor a D-level club in each of two Class D leagues. He had in mind the New York–Pennsylvania League and the old North Carolina State League as strong possibilities because of the compactness of the cities in those leagues and the consequent low travel costs.[32]

Rickey, the recognized master of player development for nearly forty years, had a proposal of his own, one that was at the same time radical and conservative—radical only in the sense that it was different; conservative in that he was not recommending as many league affiliations as some of the owners. In mid-January 1960 he told the third-league owners that he had plans for two Class D leagues and one Class

C league: one of the leagues would be in North Carolina; one might be the Class D Georgia-Florida League, which operated from 1935 onward but had gone out of business after the 1958 season. The other might be the Evangeline League, which had operated at the Class C level from 1949 to 1957 but had folded after the latter year.[33] What Rickey had in mind was for the Continental League, as a league or unit, to sign players and put them in a pool. These players would then be picked by lot by teams in each of the leagues he mentioned, according to the talent level of the players and the needs of each of the teams. Each league would be entirely controlled by the Continental League, and all players would be under the control of the league as a whole. When players were ready to advance to the Continental League itself, they would be made available in a draft to all the clubs. This was different from anything seen before in Organized Baseball. Was it socialism, an economic system that Rickey, as a staunch Republican, deplored? It was certainly a kind of sharing that Rickey himself would have considered, in an earlier era, anathema in baseball.

How to start with Minor League player development was thus a key question the Continental League had to answer in early 1960. A fortuitous development, or set of favorable circumstances, led to affiliation of the Continental League with the Western Carolina League, which would become the new league's first, and only, Minor League.

4

The Western Carolina League

In the fall of 1959, a delegation of prosperous businessmen in several western North Carolina cities came to visit John Moss in Kings Mountain. The group, all of them
baseball enthusiasts with experience in the game, wanted
to explore the feasibility of reviving the Western Carolina
League, which had operated as a successful Class D circuit
from 1948 through 1952. Because Moss had helped organize the league in 1948 and had been its president during
that season, members of the delegation considered him the
logical choice to assist in their efforts. Their decision was
not only logical but wise.

John Moss was an important figure in the history of baseball, a leading light for the Minor League game for nearly
half a century. Born in Kings Mountain, North Carolina,
in 1918, he was the youngest child of a mother who died
in childbirth; his grandparents raised him. His grandfather
was a prominent member of the local community who had
settled in Kings Mountain in 1870 and went on to become
a subcontractor and builder of textile mills in the area. John
got his interest in baseball and his ability to play the game
from his father, who was an outstanding pitcher in Cleveland County, North Carolina.

Young Moss played baseball through high school in the midthirties, then as a light-hitting second baseman signed a Minor League contract with the Washington Senators. He went to spring training with other Senators' Minor Leaguers but did not play professional baseball beyond that one spring. He returned to Kings Mountain and played semipro ball until World War II, when he served in the military. During the war he attended New York University for a time, majoring in business, but did not complete a degree. After the war he came back to his hometown to work and play more local baseball. He also became a leader in organizing a prominent, high-quality semipro league in the area.

The mid- to late 1940s were a halcyon time for Minor League professional baseball, with leagues proliferating across the country, until in 1949 at peak numerical strength, fifty-nine leagues became part of Organized Baseball. Nearly every town of a population approximating ten to fifteen thousand had a local ball club. Moss's organizational skills, not to mention his affability and his uncommon common sense did not escape notice among baseball people in his area of North Carolina, and when sports-minded community leaders organized the Western Carolina League in 1948 they turned to him to become league president. He accepted the offer and at age twenty-nine became the youngest league president in Minor League history. The Western Carolina League, a Class D circuit, prospered under his direction in 1948, then went on to four more years of operation until it folded after the 1952 season.

In 1949 Moss received an offer of more money and a chance to run a ball club when the owner of the Rock Hill, South Carolina, franchise in the Class B Tri-State League asked him to take the position of business/general manager of the team. Rock Hill operated independently, that is to say, did not have direct affiliation with a Major League organization, but finished fourth in an eight-team league and drew an astonishing ninety-eight thousand fans. That was greater attendance by a considerable margin than the St. Louis Browns of the American League had drawn during two separate years in the 1930s.

Moss's success at Rock Hill quickly attracted the attention of Major League organizations, and in 1950 he received an offer from the Detroit Tigers to become business manager of their ball club in Jamestown, New York, in the Class D Pony League, a circuit comprised of eight small cities in northern Pennsylvania and upstate New York. Despite the team's sixth-place finish in an eight-team league, good work there resulted in the Tigers moving him to Richmond, Indiana, in the Ohio-Indiana League in 1951, another league at the same level but one struggling to stay afloat. Moss's efforts aside, the Richmond club drew only twenty thousand fans, and the league folded after that season.

In 1952 Moss moved to Wausau, Wisconsin, the Tigers' affiliate in the Class D Wisconsin State League, a position he held through the 1953 season. The Tigers provided good players, and Wausau finished a strong second both seasons. In 1953 and 1954 he broadened his horizons by accepting the position of business manager of the Wausau minor league professional football team. In 1955 he returned to Kings Mountain with his wife, Elaine, a farm girl from the Wausau area whom he had met at a local baseball game in 1953. Back in North Carolina, he become a public relations official and then vice president of the International Safety Corporation, a Minneapolis company that managed safety operations for a number of businesses.

Moss's reputation as a baseball man was well established, making him the natural choice as a leader when the aforementioned group began considering a reorganization of the Western Carolina League in 1959. Their contact with Moss and Moss's creativity laid the foundation for the new-era Western Carolina, Western Carolinas, and eventually South Atlantic Leagues. (Moss went on to serve as president of these organizations until 2008.)[1] Moss attended the organizational meeting for the WCL in 1959 in Gastonia and then a later meeting at which representatives of the new league elected him president. The eight cities in the league were Gastonia, Hickory, Lexington, Newton-Conover, Rutherford County (Forest City), Salisbury, Shelby, and Statesville.

Moss related to me how he helped transform the newly reestablished organization in Carolina into an adjunct of the emerging third Major League. After I had completed an article on the Continental League and forty-four years after I played in the Western Carolina League, it occurred to me in the fall of 2004 that I should determine if Moss was still alive and connected to baseball. I found a phone number on the Internet for a John Moss in Kings Mountain. The ensuing conversation went as follows: "Hello, Mr. Moss; would you happen to be the John Moss who was president of the Western Carolina League in 1960?" "I am," he said. "Well," I then replied, "you wouldn't remember me, would have no reason to do so, but my name is Russ Buhite. I am a professor of history at the University of Missouri-Rolla, and I played in the league during that season." "Hell, yes, I remember you," he answered. "You are in our record book; you were a first baseman-outfielder, a good line drive hitter and I recall seeing you throw out a runner at third base from center field in a game at Gastonia."[2] I gulped, and then asked if on my next trip to North Carolina, he would be available to talk with me about how, specifically, his league—his and mine—had made its connection to Branch Rickey and the Continental League. He immediately agreed, and thus began a friendship that continued until his death in 2009, a friendship built on mutual respect and reinforced during many lunches at Bridges Barbecue in Shelby and at least seven lengthy visits in his home.

Among other things this is what he told me about the events in the winter and spring of 1959–60. With the ownership of clubs in the various cities firmly established, owners well enough set financially to assure the league's stability, the next step would have to be locating of players. To get players of professional caliber, those who had been identified and signed by Major League scouts, it would be necessary to arrange working agreements with Major League organizations. To that end and purpose, Moss in December 1959 went to the winter baseball meetings in Miami. While there, he made contact with George Trautman, president of the National Association of Professional Baseball Leagues (then the governing body of Minor League Baseball), an old friend of Moss's dating back to 1948. Trautman agreed to introduce him to the so-called farm directors of the Major League clubs—the directors of Minor League operations—at a joint meeting. "Gentlemen," Trautman said, "this is John Moss. He wants to present the eight clubs of the newly formed Western Carolina League for your consideration for working agreements." "John," he continued, "tell 'em about it." Moss then told the assembled group about the cities in the league, the owners, the ballparks, and what outstanding baseball country North Carolina had always been. When he finished, for those who did not know, Trautman commented on what a great baseball man Moss was and how promising his league seemed to be. Then he asked for a show of hands of "those who would like to talk about putting working agreements in the Western Carolina League." Not a single hand went up, not too surprising in an era when Major League clubs were cutting back on Minor League affiliations. Increasingly, Major League clubs were limiting their signings to "can't miss" quality players, in the hope of reducing their need for developmental teams—and their costs.

Moss was disappointed, visibly so to Trautman, who told him, "I'm going to meet with these boys again day after tomorrow. If you can come back and talk with them again, you might have more success." Moss agreed. He made another presentation. Again he got no takers. As he left the meeting, he told the group that the Western Carolina League was going to operate "with them or without them" and if he or anyone in the league could be of assistance at any time to let him know: "You are always welcome in our ballparks."

The bravado aside, Moss at that point had obvious concern about stocking the clubs in his league with quality players. He went back home and contacted the owners with an idea. Like everyone in baseball, he knew about the new league developing under the leadership of Branch Rickey. Why not call Rickey and ask about a relationship with the Continental League? He quickly got Arthur Mann, Rickey's assistant, on the phone. He introduced himself and asked if he could speak to Mr. Rickey. When Rickey came on the line, Moss told him about the cities in the Western Carolina League and his interest in coming to New York to discuss a working arrangement with the Continental League. Rickey was immediately interested, knowing as he did that North Carolina was good baseball territory. Of the cities in the Western Carolina League, he said, "I've been in them all." He agreed to meet Moss in New York the following week.

It was in that meeting at Rickey's office in Manhattan that Rickey, along with some of the officials of the Continental League and Moss, established the ties between the incipient third Major League and the Western Carolina League. Present at the meeting, which began at 4:00 PM on a Monday afternoon, were Rickey; Arthur Mann; Joan Payson; Dwight "Pete" Davis Jr., son of the wealthy sportsman who originally funded tennis's Davis Cup; and Charles Hurth, a relative of Rickey, former president of the Southern Association, and soon to be named general manager of the New York Continental League club. (Earl Mann, whom Rickey had wanted for that job, did not wish to move to New York.) The meeting lasted until 8:00 p.m. and then resumed after dinner. At 2:00 a.m. Rickey, Arthur Mann, and Moss adjourned to the hotel where all three men were staying. As Moss got off the elevator, he turned to Rickey and said he expected to have something concrete to take back home and asked if they could meet the following day to finish the deal. Rickey responded, "We have concluded the deal, John. I'll send you confirmation in writing." They shook hands on the arrangement and bid one another good night.[3]

Dwight Davis initially became Rickey's envoy to the Western Carolina League. He attended a meeting with WCL officials in Newton, North Carolina, in mid-January 1960, which he then followed up with a firm commitment approved by Rickey and all the Continental League clubs on March 4, 1960, officially stating that the Western Carolina League would be the initial player-development organization. This Minor League circuit became the choice over the New York–Pennsylvania League for several fundamental reasons: the weather in that area of North Carolina was ideal for baseball; the cities were fairly close together, minimizing travel costs and eliminating expensive overnight stays; each city had an existing Minor League ballpark or its equivalent; its owners were financially solid; the managers in the process of being hired had extensive professional baseball experience and were native North Carolinians; the state was widely known for its knowledgeable baseball fans; the number of lower Minor League clubs that had operated there over the years was greater than in any other state in the nation; and Rickey, when he was with the Cardinals, had working agreements with ball clubs in the area.

The deal that Rickey and Davis put together for Moss, and that was approved by the Western Carolina League owners, was fairly generous financially. It called for the Continental League to provide each of the Western Carolina League clubs with a subvention of $7,500 for player salaries and an additional $7,500 each for spring training, the manager's salary, and upkeep of facilities. In other words, each club would get $15,000, which it would add to ticket revenue and whatever income it derived from outfield signs and other sources. If the $15,000 figure seems ridiculously low, it must be noted that the total would come to over $150,000 in today's dollars. Total subsidy going directly to the teams in the league was $120,000, or, once again, about $1,200,000 when adjusted for inflation.[4]

Beyond support for the ball clubs, Rickey hired his old friend Burt Shotton to scout players in the league and supervise managers. Shotton had been an outfielder with the St. Louis Browns and the Cardinals and then manager of the Philadelphia Phillies, the Cincinnati Reds and, in the late 1940s, the Brooklyn Dodgers. Shotton, an avuncular, soft-spoken man, was seventy-four years old and living in retirement in Florida when he was hired. Rickey paid him one thousand dollars per month, starting on May 15.

Rickey also agreed to pay Al Todd one thousand dollars per month to evaluate players, "to separate the sheep from the goats," in Todd's own phrasing. Todd had been a Major League catcher for the Phillies, the Pirates, the Dodgers, and the Cubs in the 1930s and early 1940s—a good receiver and proficient hitter, a solid Major League player who compiled a .276 lifetime batting average. He had a gruff but kindly manner and enjoyed ragging players for not using the heavy bats utilized by the "real" men of his day. Both Shotton and Todd received expenses as well as salary. A local scout from North Carolina named Harvey Stratton, who also served as baseball coach at Catawba College in Salisbury, drew a salary of four hundred dollars per month to assist in evaluating talent.[5]

Although the financial part of the Continental League–Western Carolina League connection became clear early on and was fairly easily arranged, the acquisition of players for the new Minor League remained more complicated. Since none of the Continental League clubs had signed any players, they had none to send to North Carolina. So two approaches developed, both consistent with Rickey's prior experience: Each Western Carolina League club was encouraged to reach out to young free-agent players, to a few veteran players who had retired from baseball, but more especially to young men who had had professional experience, once considered excellent prospects, but who had been released before they could realize their potential. The latter was not an unusual occurrence in a baseball world in which the number of Minor Leagues had shrunk over a decade from well over fifty to just over twenty. The other approach was to identify talent the way Rickey had done for years: through the tryout camp. The Continental League and the wcl placed advertisements in newspapers seeking free agents—college players, semipro players, and others who wanted to play professional baseball—to come to tryouts to be held in Newton and Gastonia in April. Continental League player evaluators, namely, Todd, Shotton, and

Stratton, but for a time Rickey himself, participated in assessing this talent. Beginning rosters were set in this way. But as the Western Carolina League season neared and all the clubs in the Continental League moved forward, those clubs began signing promising young players and assigning them to the WCL.

But herein lay a problem. Commissioner Frick began a round of gamesmanship. He informed John Moss that the WCL could not be a part of Organized Baseball if it were connected to the Continental League because the latter was not itself a part of Organized Baseball. Then he argued that Rickey's proposed league-to-league arrangement for player assignment and the overseeing of WCL business violated the rules of Organized Baseball. Frick's position was that until the Continental League satisfied the territorial rights issue, the Continental League clubs proposing to operate in cities that already had Minor League teams could not be admitted to Organized Baseball.

At this point at least, the WCL did not want to operate outside Organized Baseball, and Frick's admonition threw officials and owners in North Carolina into a quandary: they might have to fold up before even starting. Frick's maneuvering set Rickey off: "Show me the rule," he thundered at Frick about the league-to-league assignment and evaluation of players: "There is no such rule." A furious Rickey remonstrated that the National and American League clubs were refusing to alter the reserve clause, which worked to deny the Continental League the opportunity to obtain players, and now they were attempting to prevent the new league from developing players on its own. That Frick, in fairness to him, may have been correct in the long term that in order to avoid conflicts of interests, league-to-league arrangements and the pooling of players were not good ideas, in the short run his "rule" clearly interfered with a timely advancement of the new league's establishment. What Frick hoped to do was harass the Continental League into giving up.

Rickey's answer was twofold. He and his new associates began pulling strings. They arranged for Senator Kefauver and Senator Everett Jordan of North Carolina to meet with Frick about the Western Carolina League, thereby putting enormous pressure on the commissioner, especially given the pending legislation concerning the reserve clause. Nearly simultaneously, on April 18 Rickey appeared on television station WNEW in New York to announce that the Continental League was prepared to operate independently and sign as many players on National and American League rosters as it desired. It would "raid" the Major Leagues. This dual activity scared the owners, as it did Frick, who devised a fig-leaf solution: if the Western Carolina League teams would apply as independent clubs to the National Association, they could be admitted to Organized Baseball. Once they had taken that step, each of the Continental League clubs could make a working agreement with a Western Carolina League city. That is exactly what transpired. But it did not stop Rickey from pursuing league-to-league arrangements of various sorts. Indeed, all important decisions about support for the WCL, player development, and evaluation, originated in Rickey's office, because the Continental League teams as yet had little identity or autonomy. All Frick's ploy did was delay the start of the WCL season until May 25.[6]

Although in some ways these working agreements may have seemed fictional, in other ways they were very real. The latter was the case if the Continental League was one and the same, with the same ownership, as the one already operating in Organized Baseball. Such was the case with

Denver. Denver's owner, Bob Howsam, concluded a working agreement with the Rutherford County ball club (Forest City) in which Denver provided $1,500 a month to the owner of the Rutherford County club, Bruce Greene, in return for which Denver got the right to all players on the club. Denver could assign all players as it wished; it could take as many players as it wished the following season. Moreover, no release or other assignment of players could occur without Denver's (meaning Bob Howsam's) approval; and the selection of the manager, or his dismissal, had to be determined in Denver. A further proviso was that Denver, at season's end, would pay Greene $7,500 to cover losses, if such a payment were needed.[7]

By that route, or in any case through a circuitous route, I became "property" of Denver of the Continental League, if the Continental League became a viable venture, or of Denver of the American Association if the Continental League never came to fruition. As previously noted, I played for Forest City during the 1960 season. Bill Harris, the veteran Major League pitcher who had pitched for Cincinnati, Pittsburgh, and the Boston Red Sox in the 1920s and 1930s and who was the Washington Senators' scout who had signed me in 1959, recommended me to Jim Poole, the manager at Forest City, and Bruce Greene, the owner. Harris thought I was a prospect and believed I had not received decent treatment in the Washington Minor League system, which was in serious disarray in 1959.

In April 1960 Bruce Greene called and then mailed me a contract for the 1960 season. Greene was the owner of a successful feed and farm supply store and a chicken hatchery in Forest City. He was a good, decent man, without question the most caring and generous of any owner I ever played for in professional baseball, and he also became a good friend. I did not participate in the so-called spring training sessions at Newton and Gastonia and instead reported directly as soon as I completed my college final examinations. I arrived shortly after May 1 in Forest City, where the ball club, with a few additions as assigned from Denver, was pretty well set.

In some respects the Western Carolina League was a Class Double-A or Class A league; in some respects a Class D league (its formal classification); in all respects it was a quality league, given the many experienced players on the various clubs' rosters. Rickey did not consider letter classification or stratification a critical issue. He wanted both experienced and inexperienced players in the league, and he did not believe in lockstep advancement to the top. Some players in this original Continental League Minor League circuit might be—as his player evaluators and he himself later stated—only one step away from Major League status.

In 1960 and for many years prior to 1960, the cities in this Minor League were, though not large in population, well known for interest in baseball. The largest cities were Gastonia, with a 1960 population of around 30,000; Salisbury with slightly under 20,000; and all the others, except Forest City, with between 12,000 and 18,000 people. Rutherford County, with its ball club located in Forest City, had about 50,000 residents, while Forest City itself had fewer than 7,000. All the cities were within easy driving distance of one another, making it possible to play an away game, then return within a couple of hours to the home city. In fact, much of the schedule involved home and away games on back-to-back nights with the same opponent. Teams traveled by car, station wagon, and bus; the Lexington club had the most unappealing but eye-catching vehicle: a 1946 Chevrolet school bus. In Forest City we traveled by car, one of which was Jim Poole's 1953 black Cadillac, which he always asked me to drive—it was a comfortable, spacious vehicle that would seat five players.

Players found in these small Carolina cities what they were wont to find. New Yorkers at first found them oppressive, too tranquil, and lamented their inaccessibility to Coney Island. Others possessed varying expectations, depending on their experience or their places of origin. There were striking similarities among the cities. Drive-in restaurants where one could get a variety of sandwiches and beer abounded in this era predating most national fast-food chains. The downtowns all had small cafés, some of them run by snuff-dipping, middle-aged women who looked after a regular clientele but doted on the local ballplayers as well. It was possible to get a substantial stack of pancakes at most of these establishments for 35 cents. Coffee cost a nickel or a dime; Coca-Cola a nickel. Sweet iced tea must have been free because it was everywhere, at all times of day and night. Bacon, eggs, grits, and coffee went for 55 to 60 cents. Lunch with the blue-plate special—often fried chicken or cubed beef, a vegetable, "slaw" (slaw never seemed to count as a vegetable), and French fried potatoes—was 79 cents. Dinner would run to $1.25 or $1.50, depending on the choice. Outside the city limits were "fish camps," usually clapboard, barnlike buildings where one could load up on as much catfish, French fries, hush puppies, slaw, and banana pudding or peach cobbler as one could hold. Each city had a fancy restaurant or two, some of them barbeque places that served up the most delicious pork barbeque sandwiches in the nation. All cities had their small drugstores, where the soda fountain and the candy counter were featured attractions. In Forest City most ball players ate and gathered at Smith's Drugstore, still very much a fixture in the heart of town.

The downtown areas were vibrant. Because there were no shopping centers, small retail stores seemed to thrive. Most of the proprietors went to ball games. As an added benefit, some store owners offered prizes, merchandise of some sort, to players who excelled in particular games. A four-hit night, a key home run, a well-pitched game, could bring a new shirt, a couple pairs of underwear, some fancy new shoes. Downtowns were dotted with pool halls as well, popular places for ball players to congregate during their off hours. And every town had two or three movie theaters.

The civil rights movement had not yet gained ground in the Western Carolina League cities. Racial segregation was pervasive, and the evidence of it was startling to those of us accustomed to a greater degree of racial tolerance. African Americans were relegated to theater balconies. Blacks were derogatorily referred to as "Nigras," with separate "Nigra" schools, homes, towns, and taverns. Blacks sat in the back of buses, used separate restrooms, ate in the back rooms of restaurants with the black cooks and black waiters. At ballparks black patrons sat in separate bleachers, always along the left-field line. Black players roomed in homes in the black section of town and seldom associated with white players off the field.

The local ballparks were good, if not outstanding. In five of the communities the cities themselves owned the parks. In two of them the local American Legion post was the owner, and in Salisbury Catawba College owned the facility. Gastonia, which had had a Class A team (and would be in Class A ball again later), possessed the best grandstand and field. Newton had a fairly large, old wooden grandstand, of a prototypical lower Minor League variety, that would seat 2,500 to 3,000 fans, counting the segregated bleachers. Its field was adequate but not properly manicured. Incredibly, the Newton club eleven years before had drawn an amazing 82,481 people to its Western Carolina League games.[8] The most unusual playing surface was in Lexington, where a steep incline ran up to the outfield wall in left and left-center fields, an embankment extremely hard for an outfielder to navigate. All the parks had adequate lighting, with Gastonia the best and Hickory the worst. Of the locker rooms or clubhouses, Gastonia, Newton, and Lexington were the most commodious and Forest City the least. The latter had an old grandstand and cramped quarters with inadequate showers, even for the limited rosters of players. The Statesville ballpark had a short right-field fence rising about fifteen feet from the ground about three hundred feet from home plate. Left field was far more challenging. The rosters consisted of fifteen players, which meant eight regulars, six pitchers, and a reserve catcher; or seven pitchers if one of them could play another position, or catch; or if one of the regulars could do so, he would serve as the backup catcher.

The managers were well chosen. Four of them had played in the Major Leagues, two had enjoyed outstanding playing careers, and one had extensive managing experience. Jake Early, who managed Statesville, had been a Major League catcher with the Washington Senators and the St. Louis Browns for nine years, the best of which was 1941, when he had hit .287. Possessed of a strong arm and perhaps best known in his time for having picked Ted Williams off third base twice in the same game after Williams had twice tripled, Early, by his own admission, in his playing days was also known as "bad to drink." He once admitted that he had mastered the art of catching with his left leg stretched out straight as a prop, for balance, after his drinking bouts. And he also noted that when Ellis Kinder, a man of similar taste in beverages, was pitching and he was catching for the Browns, the combination was dangerous to everyone's health. Rickey liked Early, a genuinely nice fellow and a true gentleman, because he had by 1960 given up alcohol. Early managed and played for Statesville until a dispute with the owner led to his dismissal in late July.[9]

Jim Poole, who managed Forest City, was a gentle, quiet man, of calm disposition, who had been in baseball as a player, a manager, and both concurrently for over forty years. He had been a power-hitting first baseman with Portland of the Pacific Coast League from 1921 through 1924, a consistent .300 hitter who annually had over 40 doubles and in 1924 led the league with 38 home runs. He played for the Philadelphia Athletics in 1925, 1926, and part of 1927, until Jimmie Foxx took his job. He hit .298 in his first full season and .294 in his second. After 1927 he went on to star at Atlanta and Nashville in the Southern Association. At Nashville in 1930 he hit 50 home runs and drove in 167 runs. During his cumulative professional career, in Major and Minor Leagues, he amassed over 3,000 hits, over 700 doubles, and over 300 home runs. As a manager he was calm, grandfatherly (then sixty-five years of age), tolerant, and understanding; his motto was "live and let live." Some players took advantage of him. I loved him and worked hard for him. Years later, when as a university professor I took my family to visit him, he repeatedly insisted that I had quit baseball far too soon, just as I was "really learning how to play." He assembled the most Major League prospects in his lineup but failed to win enough games because he was too easygoing and not properly attentive to pitching instruction.

The other former Major Leaguers, both of whom played as well as managed in the Western Carolina League, were George "Teddy" Wilson, who managed the Shelby team, and Billy "Doc" Queen, who managed at Gastonia. Wilson had played for the New York Giants, the New York Yankees, and the Chicago White Sox, and Queen had played for the Milwaukee Braves, though both had spent far more time in the Minor than in the Major Leagues. Altogether Wilson played professional baseball for twenty years, compiling a .311 average with 275 home runs in the Minors. Queen played in the Minor Leagues for fourteen seasons, establishing a .277 lifetime average. He played in the Pacific Coast League in 1959.

At Hickory and Newton respectively, Joe Abernethy and John Isaac were the managers. Neither had much managerial experience, but Abernethy had managed for a short time in the Florida State League in 1959. His best playing performance had been at Missoula in the Pioneer League, where he had played several positions. Isaac was a pitcher whose best years had been in the Sally League (South Atlantic League, formed in 1904). He was twenty-five years old, a small left-hander with three or four pitches, all of which he could control. Both he and Abernethy played with distinction, Isaac leading the league in strikeouts. Both Lexington and Salisbury had former Minor League players at the helm. Jack Hale managed at Lexington and Larry Taylor at Salisbury. Each guided his team to an outstanding season. Jack Hale had been a left-handed pitcher who pitched for eight years, at one point reaching Triple-A. Larry Taylor had been a middle infielder in the Cincinnati organization for eight years. He spent five years in Double-A.

Abernethy, Early, and Poole were fired before the season ended, because either local ownership was dissatisfied with their performance, or the Continental League brass wanted a change, or both. In some cases, as in the dismissals of Abernethy and Early, Branch Rickey was not pleased, to say the least. Statesville's owner, Fleet McCurdy, dismissed Early after an argument about players, especially Early's patience with pitchers.

Bob Howsam of Denver recommended Poole's removal on the basis of age. He wanted a younger, more dynamic person in charge; and after a week with Ray Welsh, a former Pittsburgh scout in the job, he secured that dynamic fellow in Leonard Jackson, a catcher/infielder, who went on to play AAA ball the next year. Jackson played and managed, and both he and Welsh were competent, personable managers. Rickey informed Hickory's owner of his unhappiness with the firing of Abernethy but never received an adequate explanation for the action.[10]

Todd and Shotton sent their regular weekly evaluation of players and managers to Rickey's office. Managers, who were also paid one thousand dollars per month (Rickey determined all salaries), submitted weekly reports on players, though some managers reported daily. They understood with Rickey that assessment of players was not an exact science and that views could change from day to day. These reports went directly to the central office and often only indirectly to the individual Continental League clubs with which the Western Carolina League teams had working agreements.

The working agreements thus did not operate in quite the way they did elsewhere in Organized Baseball. But Bob Howsam, president of the Denver club then in the American Association, took an active interest in the team Denver sponsored, because as noted, whether the Continental League got off the ground or not, he had the "rights" to any player on the Forest City roster during and after the 1960 season; and he could influence the hiring and firing of managers. Hence, he made his presence known in Forest City during the season. Other working agreements were as follows: Gastonia, with Atlanta; Hickory, with Buffalo; Lexington, with Minneapolis-St. Paul; Newton, with Dallas-Fort Worth; Salisbury, with Houston; Shelby, with New York; and Statesville, with Toronto.

Players' salaries were a prime concern of both local ownership and the Continental League. Most players earned somewhere between $200 and $450 per month, but veteran players and a few rookie prospects made more. I made $250 per month, but when it became obvious I was having an excellent season, Bruce Greene increased the amount by $100, without my asking that he do so. Some players received contingency bonuses whereby they would receive a few thousand dollars if they were still with a given club after a set period, often thirty days. There were several veteran players in the league, some with well over five years of professional experience; some were well paid, some not. Among the rookies Jim Flowers on the Forest City club, a big, rawboned pitcher, had a contract calling for $600 per month. This caused some hand-wringing among local ownership. Some rookies, such as Flowers, were paid more to keep them from signing with National or American League clubs.[11]

In that era most of the top-quality young ball players were playing in the Minor Leagues and not in college, so the level of play was comparatively high. To succeed in the Major Leagues, most players and baseball officials believed, one had to play continuously, a hundred games a year, for years. The only place to do that was in the professional Minor Leagues.

Lexington and Salisbury possessed the best combination of players in key positions and dominated the standings throughout the hundred-game schedule, which began on May 25 and ended on September 5. Lexington had three hitters in the final top ten in batting average, and the club had a hard-throwing left-handed pitcher named Bill Bethea, who finished with the league-leading earned run average. The leading hitter was Salisbury's second baseman, Jack Turney, at .362, and the leader in home runs was Salisbury's first baseman, Paul Roberts, with twenty-three. Both teams were fairly strong in the middle infield; both had good catching and pitching. Interestingly, Al Todd reported to Rickey that Salisbury had no obvious prospects but had really good players at most positions—for that level of baseball. The team had three good left-handed pitchers in Jimmy Basinger, Kermit Daub, and Gary Henson. Henson was a soft-throwing lefty but could change speeds well and had excellent control. He won fifteen games.[12]

Hickory and Newton filled out the first division in that order. But only Hickory joined Lexington and Salisbury with a record above .500. Hickory's Danny Hayling, a dominating veteran right-handed pitcher, had extensive professional experience and served as their ace; he won twenty-two games. Newton's playing manager, John Isaac, had a good fastball, an excellent curve ball, and exquisite control. Each club had adequate hitting but played poorly on defense. The Hickory shortstop, Don Bush, who possessed one of the strongest arms in Organized Baseball, made sixty errors in eighty-nine games, while the Newton shortstop, Kenneth Orbison, committed fifty-two in eighty-six games.

Some of the other teams did well early in the season but lost their momentum later on, even though, as is often the case, these were teams with some of the more outstanding prospects. Statesville and Gastonia were never competitive and finished about twenty-five games under .500. Rutherford County (Forest City) and Shelby started out well but then began to slip as the season wore on. Statesville and

Gastonia each possessed decent hitting but had spotty pitching and inadequate defense. Forest City had five talented pitchers, two of whom had Major League fastballs. But there were only four consistent hitters and not enough run-producing power to offset poor defense. Our first shortstop, Larry Schultz, made thirty-six errors in forty-one games, and his replacement, Enrique Bonitto, made thirty in fifty-four games. Generally, our team was not strong up the middle, though our catching was quite good. Shelby had a left-handed pitcher, Darvin Moss, with an overpowering Major League fastball and a few good position players but could not move into the first division.

Among the many memorable developments of the 1960 season, two in particular stand out: one on the field and one off; one hilarious and one horrific. The hilarious came during a game at Newton early in the season. With a runner on first and two outs, our second baseman, Pat Foster, moved to his left and dropped down to field a sharply hit ground ball. As the first baseman I moved off the bag to my right toward the ball, then immediately turned back to cover first. When I looked for the throw, I instead saw Foster frantically turning in circles trying to find the ball. He quickly located it—inside his uniform shirt, in the back; it had crawled up his sleeve and slid around his torso. The runner on first went to second, then tentatively rounded the base, and moved toward third. Foster, realizing that the runner might score, ran as hard as he could to the third base line while working the baseball around to the front of his shirt. He positioned himself, ball held in two hands still inside his shirt, straddling the third base line prepared to tag the runner if he tried to advance to home plate.

While all this was happening, I began screaming, "Time out, time out," to the base umpire (Minor Leagues then used only two umpires). The umpire yelled back, "You can't call time out while the play is going on." Gary Cowan, our catcher, screamed, "Time out, time out," to the plate umpire. He yelled back to Cowan, "You can't call time out while a play is in progress." The play, as it turned out, only stopped being in progress with a runner standing on third and the hitter standing on second and our second baseman with his shirt untucked, outside his pants. When the laughter ceased, play resumed, and we got the third out. When we were safely in the dugout, I told Foster that I would hit him ground balls for as long as it took to duplicate the feat. I would hit him ten thousand if took that many; we would start the next morning. He declined, and we laughed some more. We did not win the pennant, but we put on the best show, one of the best in baseball history.

The most horrific development occurred in Gastonia. In a game between Gastonia and Lexington on July 16, one of the umpires made a call against Gastonia that manager— and player—"Doc" Queen contested vociferously and ceaselessly, on and on, using profanity that would have made a grizzled sailor blush. The umpire ejected him. Queen left the field but hid out of sight near the dugout, where he continued haranguing the men in blue, Leonard Arndt and Jim Clegg. Gastonia lost the game. After the game was over, a professional boxer named Al Cook, a Gastonia fan obviously sympathetic to Queen, broke into the umpires' dressing room and beat the hell out of the umpires, sending them to the hospital and rendering them incapable of continuing their duties, at least for a time. The assailant was arrested and sentenced to eight months in jail. John Moss fined Queen $25.00(!) and the ball club $250.00. President of the National Association George Trautman suspended Queen for ninety days, which would have continued into the next season. (Queen, who had hit a combined .312 in Double-A and Triple-A in 1959, hit .296 in the Western Carolina League in 1960.) The Gastonia owner appealed the suspension, and Queen resumed his managerial and playing assignment on August 23. The most severely injured of the umpires, Clegg, was one of the league's best, a good guy, fair-minded and friendly, and victim, as it turned out, of one of the most heinous crimes in Minor League history.[13]

In early June my parents, who had never seen me play in a professional game and who had seldom seen me play at any level, brought my wife down from Pennsylvania to join me in Forest City. My wife, Mary, an elementary school teacher who did not finish her first year of teaching until the first week in June, had not accompanied me when I joined the ball club. On the night of their arrival, they saw the final innings of our game at Shelby. The next night we played the second game of a home series at Forest City.

That game at Forest City was memorable to me. During batting practice George "Teddy" Wilson, Shelby's manager, began ragging us, especially the left-handed hitters, about the impossibility of our chances against his starting pitcher that night, his flame-throwing left hander, Darvin Moss. In front of my parents, my little sister, then thirteen years of age, and my wife, I hit two long triples against Moss. One of the hits came on Moss's best fastball, a pitch I turned on and drove to right center. The second came on a slider away that I drove to left center for the game-winning hit.

My next encounter with Moss was far less pleasurable. In our next game with Shelby some weeks later, Moss hit me in the head with his best fastball, a pitch that I had no doubt the manager Wilson ordered Moss throw, because that was the way he played the game. Moss's control was not good enough to knock me down, which he and Wilson probably wished to do, without hitting me. The next day Jim Poole and Al Todd both submitted reports to Rickey about the beaning; Poole commented: "Buhite was hit in the helmet last night; it didn't seem to bother him." Needless to say, as all my teammates were aware, it bothered me; the pitch cracked my batting helmet.

My best all-round performance came near the end of July during a game at Statesville. I made several good plays in left field and went 4 for 4 at the plate, including a walk and a double off the right-field wall that drove in the deciding run. That was the same game in which my teammate Joe Priestes hit the longest ball I had ever seen hit that did not leave the park—a triple to the far reaches of left-center field.

Apart from the inadvertent hidden ball trick by our second baseman, the most amusing incident involving my own play came in a midseason game with Hickory. I had played for a couple of weeks with excruciating pain in my left (throwing) shoulder, which I mentioned to no one, but which a local orthopedist diagnosed as bursitis. I could throw all right when playing first base, but a long throw from the outfield just killed me. Hickory had a runner on second when the hitter drove a ground ball single to left field. I charged the ball hard and made my best, but pained-filled, throw to the plate. Our third baseman for some reason did not cut the ball off, and it took about fifteen bounces before it got to our catcher, my good friend Gary Cowan. The ball arrived at exactly the same time as the runner, who smacked Cowan as hard as a linebacker hitting a receiver in the open field, rolling him backward a minimum of ten feet. Cowan got up still holding the ball for the out but spitting pebbles and dirt from his bloodied lips, his chest protector ripped to one side. As we ran to the dugout, he shouted every obscenity in his not inconsiderable vocabulary at me. My response was, "Quit your fucking bitching; the ball got there; it just took a little longer than usual." He quickly cooled off, and we laughed about the play the rest of the season. We laughed about it again when I met him—now a distinguished lawyer in Colorado Springs—for a round of golf fifty-one years later.

The season ended with Lexington first, Salisbury second, Hickory third, and Newton fourth; under the playoff plan, Lexington played Hickory, and Salisbury played Newton. Hickory defeated Lexington, and Salisbury defeated Newton, each in a three-game series. Salisbury then beat Hickory three games to two in the final. Lexington had by far the best season record at seventy wins and twenty-nine losses but did not emerge as the playoff champion.[14]

For many of the players, however, these results meant little. By the time the 1960 Western Carolina League season ended, the Continental League had effectively drawn its last breath. Meanwhile, we watched with keen interest as Congress determined our fates.

After a year of political maneuvering, the antitrust subcommittee of the Senate Judiciary Committee, under the chairmanship of Senator Kefauver, had recommended passage of a bill that would have changed the business of baseball and supported the Continental League. The Senate began debate on the legislation earlier that summer on June 28, 1960, amid strong opposition from the baseball establishment. As previously discussed at length, after numerous amendments and emendations, the bill was finally remanded back to the Judiciary Committee, without an up or down vote on its merits. It could not be brought up again in that session of Congress, nor would doing so have made any difference. Given the talk of expansion by the National and American Leagues, which soon resulted in the addition, in 1961 and 1962, of two new clubs in each of those leagues, the Continental League was, for all intents and purposes, dead. Reginald Taylor, owner of the Buffalo Continental League club, was quoted in the *Sporting News* on July 6 as saying that unless the Kefauver bill were reconsidered, the Continental League had no chance of operating. A National League club official leaked a story to the *Sporting News*, published in the July 20 issue, that both the National League and the American League planned to expand to ten teams by 1962. Then, on July 27, the National League expansion committee, consisting of Walter O'Malley, John Galbreath, Lou Perini of Milwaukee, and Bob Carpenter of Philadelphia, announced that just as soon as the Continental League was declared officially defunct, both American and National League expansion plans would proceed. This statement guaranteed that the Kefauver legislation would not reappear.[15] Only though modification of the reserve clause could the Continental League get enough players to operate in the short run. My teammates and I read the *Sporting News*; we were aware of this fact. The Continental League had put my baseball aspirations on life support; now I would give up baseball and go on to graduate school and pursue another career.

Organized Baseball had based its argument for no restriction on the reserve clause and against an unrestricted draft on one major point. Unless Major League clubs could sign players and retain them as long as they wished, they would have no incentive to develop talent, to support Minor League teams. Major League support was critical to the survival of those teams; passage of the bill would inevitably kill the Minor Leagues. The argument had a jarring effect, and it was not easily refutable by the founder of the farm system. That it was untrue or at best half true no one effectively brought out.[16]

As the Western Carolina League season came to a close, Rickey compiled a final assessment of talent—a list of players who were either "prospects" or had "money value." Players with "money value" could be sold to Major League organizations before they were "seized"—drafted—for as little as $12,500 each. These players had money value through the draft or through sale because they were "owned" by the Western Carolina clubs in the National Association, which were part of Organized Baseball, or they were the "property" by virtue of working agreements, of Continental League franchise clubs then in Organized Baseball. The Continental League might not have received an official imprimatur as part of Organized Baseball, but the Western Carolina League had, and so the players had as well.

The "talent" list of thirty-three names included seven pitchers, numerous infielders and outfielders, and five catchers. Rickey noted that Bill Bethea, left-hander of Lexington, "could go to the major leagues right now" and could be worth $250,000. (Bethea probably could have pitched in the Major Leagues in 1960 but for unknown reasons never made it there.) Rickey's signing of Jackie Robinson integrated baseball, but he still identified African American players as "colored" or "Negro" and often singled out stereotypical traits. For instance, he referred to Bethea as "bootblack," a "mollycoddle," a "pin cushion," a "boy" with "fingers long, hands big." He allowed managers to submit reports such as one sent in by George Wilson about Don Bridges saying, "My colored boy pitched a real fine game." Rickey's assessment of playing talent was accurate, however, as he identified in each case arm strength, running speed, hitting skills, and attitude. Bethea, incidentally, had done nothing to diminish his evaluation with a complete game, eighteen-inning performance against Forest City in which he struck out twenty-five batters.[17]

Forest City had eight players on Rickey's list. I was not one of them, but I did lead the club with a batting average of .303 and was selected to play in both of the leagues' All-Star Games. The evaluations of me that Todd and Shotton submitted included comments such as "hustles all the time," "well-built boy," "good everyday player," pluses in most categories and double-pluses for running speed; their notes read: "good hitter without power"; "only fair power"; "prospects: AA." All the evaluations were correct, both those submitted during the season and Rickey's final evaluation. As a left-handed first baseman/outfielder without power, I was probably not a Major League prospect. That is to say, I was probably not a prospect for the existing Major League clubs. Whether I would have eventually become a Continental League player is an open question.[18]

Rickey's interpretation of Major League talent is interesting and insightful: "Who is to say what constitutes a major leaguer? Is Willie Mays the only major league player on the San Francisco club? There are twenty-four others. They are not Willie Mays but they are major leaguers." "You'd be surprised," he opined further, "how many players are around and how quickly they'd develop." During the struggle to organize the Continental League, he observed that Major League clubs annually signed between thirty and forty players, only two or three of whom made the Major Leagues. Rickey, Todd, and Shotton believed, and all the Western Carolina League managers agreed, that the league proved his point about player development: if given a chance and a place to play, year after year, many players who were too soon released because of the dwindling number of Minor League teams could go on to the Major Leagues.[19]

Had the Continental League begun to operate as its leaders intended, with eight ball clubs playing only against one another for a two- or three-year period, many of the players in the 1960 Western Carolina League with another year or two of experience could have, without question, made the rosters of Continental League teams. There was superb talent in the WCL. In Forest City we had Leonard Jackson, then only twenty-six years of age, a six-feet-two, 210-pound catcher with six years of professional experience who could throw with anyone who ever played the game, was a fine receiver and an excellent hitter. He played at Columbus in the International League and at Charlotte in the South Atlantic League the following year. For the final month of the season at Forest City, he also proved to be a highly effective manager. We also had Gary Cowan, a left-handed hitting catcher, a fine receiver with an excellent arm who hit .283 for the season. He stood six feet four, weighed 190 pounds, and was a quality all-round athlete, capable of playing other positions.

In the outfield we had two or three players who might have made the Continental League itself. George Ferrell, son of George S. Ferrell, a former longtime Minor League player, manager, and scout, and nephew of Major League stars Rick and Wes Ferrell, had been a bonus player with Detroit. He had injured himself the previous year when he ran into a concrete outfield wall in spring training but had recovered and was a fine player for us. At six feet three and 180 pounds, with a good arm, excellent speed, and a powerful left-handed bat, he could have had a long career in a third Major League. He hit .294 for the season. Troy Searcy from nearby Lake Lure, North Carolina, was a strong left-handed hitter who had serious power and a strong throwing arm. In any prior era he would have been a much-coveted Major League prospect. Joe Priestes, who also played the outfield, was the first player I ever knew to work with weights. He had excellent home run power, a strong arm, and drew attention from all the scouts following the league.

Among pitchers on our club were two or three who, barring injury, could have made it. Gene Garnell, a strong right-hander, had a fastball that must have ranged from ninety to ninety-five miles per hour. He went on to play eight more years, several in Triple-A. Jim Flowers, another right-hander, threw nearly as hard. Ray Searcy, our ace, had a live fastball and a sharp breaking curve ball. He finished the season 14-16 with a 2.67 earned run average in 246 innings pitched.

We had two players on the Forest City Ball club who possessed backgrounds that Rickey especially admired. Willie MacDonald, a second baseman, had been a star baseball and basketball player at Lafayette College, and an economics major. He hit only .229 but showed some power and enough promise to receive an invitation to the Detroit Tigers spring training camp in 1961. Tommy Jamieson, a left-handed pitcher from Pfeiffer College, where he had gone undefeated for three full seasons and regularly made the dean's list (he majored in chemistry), achieved a 5-1 record for us as a reliever. He stood only five feet seven and weighed no more than 140 pounds. His size did not concern Rickey, however, who knew that like Bobby Shantz, the diminutive star left-hander with the Philadelphia Athletics and then the New York Yankees, Jamieson knew how to retire hitters.

On other clubs several players displayed outstanding talent. Darvin Moss, the aforementioned lefthander at Shelby, had a Major League fastball. Marc Hoy, an outfielder with Hickory could, in Rickey's words, "outrun anyone in the country." He went on to Class Double-A and Triple-A as a pitcher. Ken Free at Hickory was one of the league's leading hitters and a fine third baseman. John Isaac, pitcher and manager at Newton, ranked as a top prospect in Rickey's opinion, and mine; I could not hit him. Herby Burnette at Lexington hit .343 and played well in the outfield. Fred Green at Hickory was an outfielder who, in Al Todd's assessment, had "all the tools." Danny Hayling, then thirty years of age with several years of professional experience, led the league with a 22-9 record and a 2.00 earned run average over 229 innings. He went on to pitch for nine more years, most of them in the Class Double-A and the Triple-A Mexican League. Richard Schmidt at Newton-Conover was a first baseman who ended the season hitting .333 with fourteen triples. He repeatedly told his teammates that his ambition in life was to become a bank robber. Little did they know, as they chuckled away, that he had already begun robbing small-town banks around western North Carolina, an activity that continued after the 1960 season and eventually landed him in prison. Jim Poole told me later it was a crying shame that because there were so few jobs in baseball Schmidt had to go into robbing banks. I joined in lamenting the paucity of jobs in baseball but suggested there might have been something for Schmidt between bank robbery and baseball. Schmidt was, in fact, an excellent ballplayer who could have played at the highest level. In 1961 he played at Raleigh in the Class B Carolina League and at Mobile in the Class AA Southern Association. He hit .350 at Mobile prior to going to jail. In 1964 he came back to the Western Carolina League, because of Organized Baseball's reclassification system then an A-level league, and hit .306 in a full season with Salisbury.

All these players and too many others to mention represented the talent available to the Continental League. There were not enough players available in the WCL to stock the third Major League, but there were enough to begin doing so. The only baseball ever played under the auspices of the Continental League, it is important to note, occurred in western North Carolina. We were not Major Leaguers, would not become Major Leaguers, but we played outstanding baseball. Though we did not fully realize it at the time, we were also in some small way agents of change.

Any perspicacity about the future of Minor League Baseball on the part of the 1960 organizers of the Western Carolina League would require two decades for verification. Only in the 1980s and 1990s did the Minor Leagues make a strong comeback.

The undoing of the Continental League left the new Carolina circuit on its own for 1961 and 1962. Indeed, those years comprised a transition period for the WCL. Still a Class D league, the WCL experienced problems in acquiring players and attracting fans. National and American League clubs sent talent, but some of it was of only marginal professional quality; and an abundance of other entertainment options kept attendance low.

Forest City, Hickory, and Gastonia dropped out in 1961, creating a six-team league. Belmont, which took over the Forest City franchise, illustrates the difficulty of the 1961 season. Henry Revels, a former semipro player and baseball enthusiast from the Newton-Conover area, became the owner of the Belmont club in a cooperative arrangement with Jim Poole. Poole would be the manager and general manager, ostensibly running the operation; Revels would provide the financial backing. Poole had little money. Revels had some money, but not enough. The club operated independently at the start of the season but lost game after game. Revels feared he would dissipate his life savings. Poole had no life savings, but he knew everyone in professional baseball. In the middle of the season to bail out the operation, he asked friends in the San Francisco Giants organization to supply players and player development funds. This move helped Revels remain solvent in spite of a dismal showing at the gate: Belmont drew only 10,081 fans for fifty home games, an average of only 200 per game. Sadly, in what proved his last experience in a forty-plus-year professional career, Poole gave up the managerial duties, first to Whitey Ries, a longtime Minor League player in several organizations, and then to Max Lanier, former Major League pitcher whom the Giants sent in to take over. Belmont finished next to last with a 39-61 record. Mario Cia led the club in hitting with a batting average of .271. Barry Huntzinger was the best pitcher with a 10-9 record and a 3.72 ERA with eighty-one strikeouts.

Part of the problem at Belmont was the absence of available talent; part of it was identifying a lineup on an everyday basis. Poole and Revels had signed several players whom they controlled and hoped to see develop for eventual sale to a Major League organization. The Giants sent in players, some of whom sat on the bench while the Poole/Revels players got the bulk of the playing time. This caused friction with the San Francisco organization and ultimately led to Poole's resignation.

Poole told me about a player sent to Belmont from the Charlotte ball club. Charlotte was a longtime Washington Senators (in 1961 Minnesota Twins) Minor League affiliate in the South Atlantic League, owned by Phil Howser. In his quest for players Poole asked Howser to send him anyone not playing regularly at Charlotte who could help out at Belmont. Howser sent Tony Oliva. Poole thought Oliva could become a good hitter over time, but he did not play him because he did not like Oliva's approach at the plate: "He stood on his toes rather than planting his left foot, and he lunged at the ball." But more than that, he knew the Twins had in mind sending Oliva to the Appalachian League, to Wytheville, as soon as that circuit opened in June. Poole later expressed his surprise to me that Oliva had become a star Major League player but was characteristically generous in praising the young Cuban player's accomplishments.

No other clubs did much better at the gate. Shelby and Newton-Conover drew only 11,500 and 17,800 fans respectively. Only Statesville, the second-place club at season's end, drew over 30,000. In the split season format followed in 1961, Shelby, which had a working agreement with the Pittsburgh Pirates, won the final playoff—but made no money.

There were, however, some talented players and managers in the circuit. The managers all had extensive Major or Minor League playing experience, and all had experience as managers: Poole, Ries, and Lanier at Belmont; Aaron Robinson, former catcher for the New York Yankees, at Shelby; Alex Cosmidis, veteran Minor League player and manager, at Salisbury; George "Teddy" Wilson at Statesville; Jack Hale at Lexington; Joe Abernethy at Newton-Conover. The outstanding player in 1961 was Aaron Pointer, brother of the famous singing Pointer sisters, and later a Major Leaguer with the Houston Astros, who hit .402.

At the All-Star Game in Statesville in 1961, a contest played there because the Statesville team was in first place at the time of the game and hence under the rule the club to play against the league's All-Stars, George Wilson played everyone. His catcher, Jack Hiatt, later a Major League player, got into a row with the plate umpire, announcing after a pitch, "You dumb son of a bitch, that was a strike." The umpire not surprisingly took umbrage and threw him out of the game. Wilson had no other catchers. John Moss, who was at the game, told Wilson, "You catch." Wilson said, "Hell, I can't catch." Moss then called Hiatt over and said, "Go back in the game; you are fined $50 but go back in." Hiatt said, "I don't have $50." Moss said, "Well, find it." The umpires complained bitterly, but the game continued.

In 1962 the league's membership dropped to four teams—Statesville, Salisbury, Newton-Conover, and Shelby—and financially fell on especially hard times. Two of the clubs drew fewer than 15,000 fans each: Newton-Conover with attendance of only 10,452 and Shelby with 14,743. For a fifty-game home schedule (the league continued to play a schedule of one hundred games), that averaged out to 209 fans per contest for Newton-Conover and 294 for Shelby. That meant Newton-Conover's gate receipts per game, figured on the basis of an average one dollar per ticket, was only slightly over two hundred dollars. Those receipts would not have covered the players' payroll, not to mention other expenses. The year 1962, consequently, was the last ever in professional baseball for Newton-Conover. Only a new player development agreement the following year and heavy subsidies from Major League clubs allowed the other cities to continue.

In May 1962, because of a crisis in Minor League Baseball caused by declining attendance and a paucity of ball clubs available to develop players, the Major Leagues came up with a new player-development plan. Beginning in 1963 all Class B, C, and D leagues would be eliminated, with A thereafter the lowest classification. The South Atlantic and Eastern Leagues, previously in the Class A category, would in 1963 join the Texas League as Class Double-A leagues. Then in 1964 a newly established Southern League would replace the South Atlantic in Class Double-A. The Pacific Coast and International Leagues would continue as Class Triple-A, but the American Association, a venerable Minor League with a great history, folded. Major League clubs would pay all Class A salaries above $50 per player, all Class Double-A salaries above $150 per player, and all Class Triple-A salaries above $800 per player—based on monthly pay. Realizing the need to save the Minors, the Major League organizations agreed that at least one hundred Minor League clubs would continue to operate in 1963 and thereafter. This agreement effectively gave the Major Leagues total control over the Minor Leagues.

As the Western Carolina League adopted Class A status, it also underwent a slight name change. Spartanburg, Rock Hill, and Greenville, South Carolina, came into the league, necessitating the title Western Carolinas League. The new player-development plan and the new cities brought greater attendance and kept the WCL alive through the 1960s and 1970s, though there were rough times in the mid- and late 1970s. Dozens upon dozens of future Major League players came through the league, among them such stars as Don Mattingly, Nolan Ryan, Al Oliver, Bob Robertson, Steve Carlton, Ryne Sandberg, Dale Murphy, and Bobby Bonds.

Bonds, who played for Lexington, a San Francisco Giants affiliate in 1965, created a special problem for league president John Moss. One day Carl Hubbell, farm director for the Giants, called Moss with the unusual request that he go to Lexington and get Bonds to wear shoes. "What the hell are you talking about?" was Moss's response. Apparently, according to Hubbell, the young player liked to go barefoot off the field—all the time. So Moss went. He met with Max Lanier, Lexington's manager, at the ballpark. He said, "Max, Carl Hubbell wants you to get Bonds to wear shoes." Lanier said, "I know, I've talked to him [Bonds] all season about that." Moss called to Bonds, who had not yet put on his game uniform, and said, "Bonds, the Giants want you to wear your shoes. Look at you now. You have a cut on your foot." Bonds said, "I know, I have eight stitches, but I can still play." I asked Moss if Bonds complied with the Giants' wishes. Moss said, "Hell if I know." Despite the Giants' worries about their young prospect, Bonds was not hampered by the shoeless habit; he hit .323 with twenty-five home runs that season.

If the 1960s were a rough time for Minor League Baseball, the early to mid-1970s were in many respects even worse. Indeed, the 1970s were not a halcyon time in American history. In addition to the resignation of a president under the threat of imminent impeachment, the era brought an ignominious end to a disastrous war in Vietnam, high unemployment, double-digit inflation, unprecedented interest rates, skyrocketing gasoline prices, shortages that caused long lines at service stations, garish clothing styles—and bad music. President Jimmy Carter, as ineffectual in the presidency as he became statesmanlike in his later years, called attention to a malaise in the country. It was against this backdrop that Minor League Baseball in general and the WCL struggled to find success.

The Western Carolinas League played its last season under that name in 1979. In January 1980 league president Moss came up with an inspired plan. After the 1963 season the South Atlantic League, in existence since 1904, had folded. Many of its cities were absorbed into the newly constituted Class Double-A Southern League in 1964. Moss, an old South Atlantic League fan, urged the WCL directors to take over the South Atlantic League name and to place franchises in as many of the old "Sally" cities as possible. This move led to the dropping of the Western Carolinas League name and the beginning of the new-era South Atlantic League, a circuit that would eventually include sixteen midsized and larger cities as far north as Ohio and New Jersey and as far south as Georgia. The new Sally League became, arguably, the best run and most prosperous Class A league in the United States and sent hundreds of ballplayers to distinguished careers in the Major Leagues. Moss presided over the WCL and Sally from 1960 until 2008, when he reached ninety years of age.[20]

5

The Continental League Undercut

Historical developments often have strange endings or, if not endings, unimagined or unintended consequences. For many years leading up to 1960, public and congressional pressure had increased, demanding the inclusion of more American cities in Major League Baseball. As late as 1959, however, there seemed little movement in that direction. It took the conception and organization of a new league to bring expansion to Minneapolis-St. Paul, Houston, and new ball clubs in Los Angeles, Washington, and New York. The Continental League was thus a vehicle for dramatic change in the structure of Major League Baseball.

But the question remains whether Major League expansion through the establishment of grossly inferior teams within the National and American Leagues was the best approach, or if the Continental League, with eight admittedly talent-challenged teams playing against one another, would have worked better. The latter, both at the time and in retrospect, seems the obvious choice. That it would not have been possible, given the obstacles, to add a third league to the "horsehide cartel" seems equally obvious. For the Continental League to succeed, it had to operate independently of Organized Baseball, just as the American Football League

(AFL), which began play in 1960, kept itself independent of the NFL. Such a course would have been best for the health of baseball and perhaps for several of us personally.

The AFL, whose beginning was contemporaneous with the organization of the third league in baseball, offers an intriguing case study of what might have occurred in baseball—with some important caveats. It is not appropriate here to recount at great length the history of the new football league, but several critical events in its development, which I noted first in my 2004 article on the Continental League, are relevant. The AFL, like its counterpart in baseball, was the creation of several wealthy businessmen, most notable among them Lamar Hunt of Dallas, son of multimillionaire oilman H. L. Hunt, who led the effort.

Hunt wanted to bring a Major League Baseball team to Dallas, and he participated in at least one meeting of the Continental League owners. Content in the final analysis to see others pursue the baseball cause, Hunt turned his attention to football. As a young man of twenty-six in 1959, with lots of money and time on his hands, he had tried running batting cages and other enterprises but saw no long-term future in any of those ventures. His primary interests, though he was not particularly athletic himself, lay in sports, most especially in sports ownership. After learning that the Chicago Cardinals were in trouble financially as the second NFL franchise in Chicago—to the older, more established Bears—he flew to Chicago to see if he could purchase the team and move it to Dallas. All indications were that the Cardinals' owners wanted to sell and had no aversion to relocation. Other suitors for the Cardinals' franchise were Bud Adams of Houston, Max Winter of Minneapolis, and Bob Howsam. Hunt failed in his bid to buy the team, and so too did Howsam, Adams, and Winter. His frustration palpable, Hunt turned to Bert Bell, NFL commissioner, to see if he could help place a team in Dallas, to no avail.

On his way back to Dallas, Hunt began thinking of a scheme similar to that of Bill Shea and Branch Rickey: a totally new league. Bud Adams thought it was a good idea. So did Bob Howsam. So did Max Winter. Houston was planning a new super stadium that would need occupants in the baseball off-season (assuming that a Continental League team played there as well). Howsam already had a stadium needing off-season tenants. And the Twin Cities had a quasi–Major League park that could be made football ready without difficulty. The difference between Howsam and both Adams and Hunt was that Howsam had far less money. Winter had made his money in the restaurant business and sports promotion as well as through ownership of the Minneapolis Lakers of the NBA. Financially secure but not as rich as the Texas oilmen, and like his baseball counterparts not as devoted to the new league as its leadership, Winter would soon jump at the chance to join the more elite club, the NFL.

During the same time frame as the birthing of the Continental League—July and August 1959—the AFL began taking shape. The league held its first meeting on August 14 (and chose its name on August 22) in Chicago, where organizers granted charter franchises to Dallas, Denver, Houston, Minneapolis-St. Paul, Los Angeles, and New York. On October 28 Buffalo gained the seventh franchise, and on November 22 Boston received the eighth.

As had happened in baseball, Bert Bell as NFL commissioner at first seemed to welcome the new league, implying in fact that the new league could join the existing structure of professional football. But also as in baseball, the owners did not share those sentiments—and when in the fall Bell died of a heart attack these owners gained the ascendancy in decision making. They then sought to undercut the new league by promising franchises to Minneapolis-St. Paul (which Winter happily accepted), Dallas, and Houston. Dallas began play in the NFL in 1960 as the Dallas Cowboys, and Minneapolis-St. Paul began in 1961 as the Minnesota Vikings. When Winter and the Minneapolis group jumped ship, Oakland received that AFL franchise and became known as the Oakland Raiders.

First priority for the new league was to locate players, in some respects not as difficult as the Continental League search for talent, but not without challenges. College football produced a great many skilled, well-known players, none of them under contract to anyone, so in theory and as it turned out in practice, the AFL had a large pool from which to select. The league held its first draft on November 22, 1959, which went thirty rounds, and a second on December 2, lasting twenty. Among the outstanding players in that first round was Billy Cannon, Heisman Trophy–winning running back from Louisiana State University, who signed with Houston for a one-hundred-thousand-dollar bonus, a huge sum of money at the time. A much-coveted player, Cannon had already signed a fifty-thousand-dollar-bonus contract with the Los Angeles Rams of the NFL but did not cash the check out of concern that doing so might compromise his amateur standing and hence eligibility to play in the Sugar Bowl. Fortunately for the AFL and the Houston franchise, a judge later ruled that the Rams' management had taken advantage of Cannon's youthful innocence, and because he had not cashed the Rams' check, he was in fact the "property" of the Houston Oilers of the AFL. Cannon helped the Houston team win two of the first three AFL championship games.

Although it experienced serious growing pains, the AFL, which began its season in early September 1960, gained strength and credibility during the 1960s for a variety of reasons: it began looking to black colleges for players, a number of whom, shunned by the NFL, were truly outstanding athletes and became stars in the new league; it became known for its wide-open passing attack offenses and plenty of touchdowns; the teams, though at first inferior to those in the NFL, were playing against one another, so talent disparity did not seem glaring and each had a chance of winning the championship; and finally and most importantly, the league signed and shared equally in a lucrative television contract with ABC.

Lamar Hunt always maintained that his sessions with Branch Rickey had led to his negotiation of the television deal and his insistence that revenues be shared equally among the eight AFL teams. Rickey had repeatedly stated that Continental League owners could achieve profitability if all television income were divided equally. Hunt's initial deal, signed in June 1960 with ABC, then a network with fewer viewers than NBC and CBS, was to last for five years and called for a payment of $2,125,000 per season. Divided eight ways the deal gave each team $265,625 per year.

Apart from the money, television made a huge contribution to the success of the AFL. ABC began the practice of using unique camera angles, cameras showing close-up shots of players and of players in interviews on the field. More than that, the broadcasters themselves, among them Paul Christman, former star player at the University of Missouri and astute student of the game, who was often appropriately critical of inept play, abjured hero worship and made the games interesting to watch. His commentary along with that of his talented colleague Curt Gowdy represented the best of its time, some of the best of all time.

Perhaps foretelling what might have befallen the Continental League, the AFL experienced its share of financially unsettling times in its early years. Attendance at AFL games usually fell in the ten thousand to twenty thousand range, occasionally greater than the top figure and sometimes lower than the lesser one. Some teams did not do well financially the first year, especially Oakland, which lost over five hundred thousand dollars and only managed to survive with a four-hundred-thousand-dollar loan from Buffalo's owner, Ralph Wilson. Harry Wismer, owner of the New York Titans, found himself unable to make his payroll in the fall of 1962, and the league took over ownership of the team before selling it to a new group under the leadership of Sonny Werblin in the spring of 1963. This new group renamed the team the New York Jets.

Other such problems surrounded the league. Because of competition from the NFL Rams, the Los Angeles Chargers moved to San Diego in 1961, and for several years the Raiders in Oakland suffered from low attendance owing to the popularity of the nearby San Francisco Forty-Niners. In 1963 the Dallas Texans, Lamar Hunt's team, moved to Kansas City, where the team became known as the Chiefs, rather than compete with the NFL's Dallas Cowboys.

But play on the field was of good if not outstanding quality. And it improved each year with the addition of star college players. In one of the most spectacular moves in the league's history, the New York Jets won a bidding war for Joe Namath, who had been drafted by the NFL Cardinals, and in January 1965 signed the Alabama quarterback for $427,000. By 1966, with Oakland's Al Davis as its commissioner, the AFL began signing players already on NFL rosters, a move that drove salaries upward and caused worries in the established league.

Concerned about higher salaries and the financial impact on the older league, NFL owners, led by Tex Schramm of the Dallas Cowboys, approached AFL owners, led by Lamar Hunt, with a plan to do what all good capitalists do when faced with seemingly ruinous competition: collude. Hunt, Schramm, and other owners in 1966 began secret discussions toward a merger of the AFL and the NFL. These discussions led to an agreement between the two leagues in which in return for a payment of eighteen million dollars by the AFL to the NFL—which clearly made the AFL appear, incorrectly, as the inferior supplicant—the two leagues would begin playing championship games in January 1967 (games that would become known as the Super Bowl) and then merge completely in 1970. As all football fans are aware, the Green Bay Packers won the first two of these matchups handily, defeating Kansas City in 1967 and Oakland in January 1968. But in 1969 Joe Namath and the New York Jets upset the Baltimore Colts in one of the most surprising and important professional football results ever; and in 1970 the Kansas City Chiefs defeated the Minnesota Vikings in Super Bowl Four. After that the merger led to an expanded NFL that contained an American Football Conference and a National Football Conference, a league still in existence with additional cities holding franchises.

Whether the Continental League with different leadership and more-devoted owners could have duplicated the accomplishments of the AFL will never be known. A key difference, as mentioned previously, lay in the respective leagues' access to and control of players. The AFL standard contract contained a provision that the team originally signing a player could reserve him for the following year—or to note the euphemistic term, could exercise its "option" on him for the following year. The implication, and the practice, was that this option then could be exercised year after year, as in baseball. When owners renewed a contract, they renewed the option, so it became a perpetual option, as in baseball. As a result salaries in the AFL, with a few exceptions, were modest; star receiver Charlie Hennigan of the Houston Oilers, for instance, made only $7,500 during his first year. The AFL could sign seasoned, well-trained amateurs from the college ranks and, by virtue of the "option" clause, could keep salaries reasonably low.[1]

The Continental League certainly could have signed professional players of the highest caliber, players then under contract with National and American League clubs, at both the Major and the Minor League levels. It is doubtful that the established owners would have gone to court to defend the reserve clause out of fear for the very existence of their cartel. But how the Continental League could have disavowed the reserve clause with clean hands when it suited its purpose, knowing that its leader, Branch Rickey, would have insisted on reserving players in the new league, is an interesting question. In any event, acquiring players would prove only one obstacle to success for the new baseball league. Whatever it did, the Continental League would have earned the enmity of Organized Baseball.

There were several reasons for the opposition of the lords of baseball to the new league, some of them covered in earlier chapters, some not. One reason, previously noted, was surely Major League Baseball's reluctance to share lucrative television revenues with another eight teams, especially weaker teams that might draw smaller audiences. At the time there was widespread interest in what was then called pay television, from which the existing clubs stood to garner huge profits. Ultimately the sixteen Major League teams could, or so they hoped, telecast their games all over the country, like studio baseball. Another concern was that Continental League clubs would have better success in signing promising young players than the existing Major League clubs, because players would see correctly that their route to the big leagues would be much shorter under a Continental League contract. But this was only a part of the player problem. If eight additional clubs began bidding for young talent, they would drive up the cost of bonuses, already a significant problem in the view of many owners. Never mind that Rickey and his colleagues at first swore to pay no bonuses, then later agreed to limit any player's bonus to seventy-five thousand dollars. Regardless of original intent, doling out money for outstanding players could quickly get out of hand.

Although Major League owners did not exactly perceive Rickey as a wild-eyed extremist, they did view him as uncontrollable and too knowledgeable of their business for easy comfort, too smart for their own good. Rickey had integrated baseball. He had done so out of his belief in racial equality, if in part out of self-interest. As late as 1960 the Yankees had developed only one star black player. The Red Sox so far had no black players in the star category. In fact, throughout the 1950s the National League had come to dominate the All-Star Game because it was the more integrated of the two leagues. Rickey's talk of getting players "from the world" could mean only one thing: signing Latin American players, many, if not most, of whom were black. Owners believed that a limited number of such players would not hurt the "purity" of the game. Some of these players, such as Orestes Minoso, a Cuban player who began his Major League career with the Cleveland Indians in 1949, and Puerto Rican Vic Power, who played for the Philadelphia Athletics beginning in 1954, had made important and well-recognized contributions. But integrating baseball with players "from the world" made the owners nervous: these players were culturally different—and men of color. "Japan had not been scratched," Rickey said, a comment that could not have calmed owners' nerves, and "South Africa even."

Ford Frick and the owners further worried that Rickey might take the Continental League on an independent course, meaning that he would approve signing existing Major League players to Continental League contracts. In the short run the National and American League owners feared that the legislation sponsored by Senator Estes Kefauver might successfully limit the reserve clause, thereby helping the Continental League to recruit players. Thus far congressional legislation and the courts had favored Major League Baseball, but it was unclear whether that run of good luck would hold. A suit against the new league over its "raiding" of players would surely fail—legally ending the reserve clause. Finally, and not insignificantly, the New York Yankees firmly opposed the Continental League; they liked having a one-team town.[2]

Always profoundly ambivalent, never as enthusiastic as their leader about the third-league mode of expansion, the Continental League owners themselves were about as culpable as National and American League officials in undermining their organization. The abiding truth is that most of them wanted to become members of the exclusive club. Bob Howsam of Denver said he would not operate outside the rubric of Organized Baseball, meaning that even if Rickey opted to take the Continental League on an independent course, Denver would not come along. He announced this position even though he was a principal owner in the new—independent—American Football League.

Howsam's position was rooted in the correct assumption that the two major sports were different, mainly in their access to players. The American Football League could sign players who had had at least three years of college experience—and for many of them, experience at an extremely high level. These players were still amateurs, or technically so. The Continental League could not, Howsam believed, rely on Rickey's Western Carolina League, good as it might be, to stock Continental League rosters. It would be absolutely necessary to gain access to more-established players. Moreover, Howsam had visited the Western Carolina League more than once, and he believed there were "too many colored players" in that league, a statement of Howsam's that Jim Poole confirmed to me and Howsam made no secret of, no matter with whom he spoke. (This too is ironic, given that the American Football League, unlike the NFL, was able to build its success on the inclusion for the first time of many black players, a significant number from black colleges.) Howsam deplored Rickey's idea of getting players "from the world"; these players too would be colored, and American baseball fans would not accept them. Apart from his concern about the players, Howsam worried about the lack of respectability in going forward outside Organized Baseball. He was, after all, operating a ball club in Organized Baseball.[3]

When the National League owners held their meeting in Chicago on July 18 and followed the meeting with leaks to the press that they had voted for internal expansion, other Continental League owners began to defect—psychologically at first, then soon afterward in fact. Some had begun the psychological defection based on earlier rumors. Bill Shea said that his original mission, dating to 1957, was to get a National League team to move to New York; maybe that mission would be fulfilled, finally, by the actions of the National League. Joan Payson and her escort and accountant,

Donald Grant, who together represented the money behind the New York Continental League franchise, began to suggest that they "might be interested" if the existing Major Leagues took in four of the Continental League clubs and promised to take four more later. Roy Hofheinz, the moneyman who had taken over in Houston, expressed interest in entry into Organized Baseball, not "Outlaw Baseball." Wheelock Whitney of Minneapolis announced on July 20 that Minneapolis would cast its lot with Major League Baseball instead of the Continental League, assuming that the National and American Leagues genuinely planned to expand.[4]

Internal expansion was in fact in the offing. The National League's announcement following the July 18 meeting was itself accompanied by a telegram to the Continental League offices asking that Continental League owners and officials meet with their National League counterparts to discuss expansion—either through the third-league mode or internally. Continental League officials could determine the time and place.[5] This telegram reflected more than a little disingenuousness. The National League—and the American League as well—knew they had the upper hand, given the failure of the Kefauver legislation. At the same time, National and American League owners were mindful of the long-standing pressures from Congress and the public for expansion. Beyond that, they recognized that if in fact the Continental League went independent and raided their players, they probably had no legal recourse; they could not go to court with any confidence that the reserve clause would be upheld. So while they held the dominant position, they also had incentive to reach a settlement.

When the Continental League owners met at the Warwick Hotel in New York on July 20 to discuss the National League message, they did so with considerable anxiety.

Rickey, Shea, and several others spoke of remaining true to the new league and making a strong case to the National League owners that the third-league mode was the only sensible way to expand. But some in the group thought differently—and then there was Grant's prior comment that he "would be interested" if there were a proposal for internal expansion, whereby four of the Continental League clubs would come in immediately, with four to follow. As the meeting adjourned, the group agreed to meet with the National League owners in Chicago on August 2.[6]

At that meeting Rickey's old nemesis, Walter O'Malley, stole the show. He announced that what was best for baseball and for the country—which usually meant what was best for O'Malley—was internal expansion of the National and American Leagues. The two leagues would accept four of the Continental League franchises right away and four more later. Since this was what many of the third-league owners had come to want, and Bill Shea would get an expansion team in New York, Continental League representatives during a recess session voted unanimously to accept the offer. They accepted the deal without knowing specifically which cities would enter first and which ones later—or how much later.[7] That was the end of the Continental League, but was the arrangement best for baseball, or the country? Whether it was best for the country is hardly even a debatable question; it was, after all, only baseball. But was it best for baseball?

I am convinced that the Continental League would have been best for baseball. But to say that raises several questions about what the new league could have done, or should have done. It should have gone independent just as the American League did in 1901 and the Federal League in 1914. Rickey said repeatedly in the spring of 1960, when the Kefauver legislation seemed problematic, that if he could get just four teams to go with him, he would start an independent league. He could not get those four teams in 1960 because he had not started soon enough. He had known a year earlier, though for a long time he tried to convince himself otherwise, that the lords of baseball would not allow a third league into the existing Major League structure. He knew that officials of Major League baseball would use their powerful political friends and hints of internal expansion to defeat the Continental League. His papers are chock full of such fears. Rickey and the Continental League owners, or if not Rickey a younger leader, and if not the existing owners then others, should have announced in July 1959 that they were undertaking a frontal challenge to Organized Baseball.[8]

A frontal challenge need not have been like that of the poorly organized and funded, post–World War II Mexican League, which went independent and whose owners signed some American players, but was never, in any event, a challenge in the U.S. market. And it could have been better structured, more tightly organized, and more creative than the Federal League. Given the nation's population in 1959 and 1960, the number of boys playing baseball, the use of airplanes to reduce travel times, and the number of cities wanting Major League Baseball, the challenge through an independent approach could have been successful.

A first step beyond announcement that the Continental League would operate outside Organized Baseball should have been a statement that the new league would abide by the terms of the Sherman and Clayton antitrust laws, that it would charge its attorney or attorneys with intimate familiarity with those laws and with the task of monitoring court rulings referencing antitrust provisions. Attorneys for the Continental League, a pronouncement in July 1959 also should have said, would remain in constant contact with the Federal Trade Commission to ensure fair competition within the league and in relation to the other leagues. Consonant with rules essential to running a successful sports league, the Continental League would, as far as possible, avoid activity that restrained trade.

The Independent Carolina Baseball League, which operated in North Carolina textile towns in 1936, 1937, and 1938, offers a prime example of how the absence of firmly established rules governing the conduct of owners, players, umpires, and fans can drive a league into anarchy. This independent organization was a product of the Great Depression, which led to a severe decline in professional baseball's Minor Leagues; in 1933 only fourteen leagues still survived. Hundreds of talented ball players had no place to play in Organized Baseball. At the same time, those who had jobs in Organized Baseball, even at the highest levels, found their pay reduced to a pittance.

Baseball was so popular in North Carolina, and especially in the textile mill towns of the Piedmont region, that it had become a secular religion. Towns with textile factories found their identities through the local baseball team, and the best players on those teams became local heroes. The mills sponsored teams, with star players holding cushy jobs that required little or no work as long as the performance of players on the field remained of high caliber.

In 1936 leaders of these Piedmont communities decided to establish a professional league independent of Organized Baseball, simply elevating, by agreement, the textile league teams to professional status. The best players locally and from across the country, whether professional or amateur, would be hired exclusively to play baseball. Outstanding players were offered pay in excess of the salaries in Class

A or Double-A leagues, occasionally higher than salaries in the Major Leagues—certainly higher than what players made in Classes D, C, and B baseball. This activity led to outrage from Organized Baseball and an order from the president of the National Association, Judge William Bramham of Durham, North Carolina, blacklisting any professional player who "jumped" his contract to play in the independent league. Dozens of players jumped, nonetheless, for promises of good pay and off-season work in the textile mills. A great many star college athletes joined the league as well, knowing that in the off-season they could return to college and play there.

The league in 1936 consisted of Concord, Charlotte, Kannapolis, Valdese, Hickory, Lexington, Mooresville, and Shelby, but during the next two seasons some cities fell by the wayside and others took their place. From the outset the league was marked by fierce competition, the fiercest being that between Concord and Kannapolis; and unlike in Organized Baseball the league's purpose was not to develop players but to provide entertainment and elevate the status of the sponsoring city.

Before long, however, the fierceness, not to say the freewheeling nature of the league, led to anarchy—and after three years, its demise. Some players, having already jumped a professional contract, had no compunction about quitting one team and joining another for higher pay in midseason. Some players signed contracts for larger salaries than local ownership, usually mill owners, other businessmen, lawyers, dentists, car dealers, or others with modest money, could afford. After a year or two, the blacklist notwithstanding, some players, without warning, went on to the Major Leagues and to solid careers. Fights, brutal brawls among players and fans, became a regular occurrence. Umpires, whose authority never gained much respect, came and went. Pitchers doctored baseballs with impunity; in one case a star hurler inserted phonograph needles under the seams of a baseball used only when his team was in the field—and the activity was applauded by local owners. Anything to win became the mantra.[9]

Obviously for a professional baseball league to succeed, it had to avoid chaotic practices. Antimonopoly law was never designed to create anarchy within an enterprise. While conceding that legal minds had differed since 1890 and 1914 over the wording of the Sherman and Clayton Acts, specifically over words such as "combination" in restraint of trade, "conspiracy," "monopoly," "trust," and so on, and recognizing that few laws have ever been self-defining, Continental League owners should have announced at once that one standard practice was anathema to them and patently contrary to the meaning of antitrust law: the reserve clause in baseball players' contracts. The new league should have said it would employ no reserve clause.

The Continental League should have announced further that it would sign as many players as it wished from wherever it wished, including Major League rosters. Its teams should then have signed enough Class Double-A and Triple-A players to fill out their rosters, if for no other reason than these players were underpaid and would have come cheap. But many players on Major League rosters were making the minimum salary of seven thousand dollars— arbitrarily set by the owners—and would have been inexpensive as well. Continental League officials then should have elaborated on abjuring the reserve clause: for decent competition it would be necessary to have players under contract for a year, a stipulation surely consistent with FTC regulations, but every player at every level of baseball would become a free agent every year—unless signed to a mutually agreed-upon multiyear contract. A player, meanwhile, could be released at any time during a season, his pay either terminated or not, depending on his contract. No player's services could be sold to another club, nor could a player be traded without his permission. A system of annual free agency would have allowed the law of supply and demand to keep salaries within reason. Marvin Miller, executive director of the Major League Players Association, who helped engineer the modification of the reserve clause in 1976, always said that he opposed unrestricted free agency, preferring instead to have players dribble out onto the market in limited numbers. A few quality players available annually would lead to clubs bidding for their services and hence higher salaries; whereas if many or all players were available each year, the opposite would occur. The Major League owners in 1976 failed to see what Miller saw and thus negotiated an alteration in the reserve clause that served the players' financial interests. (The 1976 agreement provided that a Major League player became eligible for free agency only after six years of service, ensuring Miller's objective.)

If a Continental League club wished to retain a player on its Major League roster, it could sign him to a multiyear deal. If a Continental League team identified a young, free-agent prospect, a sound bet to make the Major Leagues, someone who needed Minor League seasoning, it could sign him to a long-term contract covering time for him to develop in the Minor Leagues and play for a specified period in the Major Leagues—that time to be mutually determined by the player and the club. But it seems clear that if ball clubs were aware that all, or most, players could become free agents each year, they would have had little incentive to sign players, except those with extraordinary or superstar talent, a Willie Mays or a Mickey Mantle, to long-term contracts. They would have been able to stock their rosters each year with free-agent talent at modest cost. That this would have led to players jumping from club to club year after year and hence fan disaffection seems an unfounded fear. Numerous Minor League players over the decades had returned to the same teams, for multiple years, because they came to enjoy the communities in which they played and the fans with whom they interacted—and not always because they were bound by the reserve system. The same had held true to a greater extent in semipro baseball.

Another innovative step would have been to encourage an independent players' association. Such an organization, though not dramatically effective, existed in Major League baseball and was in great measure responsible for the pension system in existence. The Continental League could have offered an improved pension system but, more especially, expressed willingness to work with a player association to address grievances that would inevitably arise.

Organized Baseball's argument that without a reserve clause the Minor Leagues would die was a canard. The Continental League would have supported Minor Leagues to develop players with long-term contracts. Players without long-term contracts would have been on the market each year and available to sign with Minor League teams. There were plenty of players wanting to play baseball. There were, in many areas of the country, people willing to pay to watch them play. This sort of free agency had worked forever in the world of semiprofessional baseball. It would have worked for the Continental League. It would have worked in professional Minor League Baseball. It would have worked for the National and American Leagues as well.

Had the Continental League put forth this challenge and then extended it, in the manner of the American Football League, the National and American Leagues could not have avoided reform. They also would have had to abide, and openly so, by provisions of the antitrust laws and the Thirteenth and Fourteenth Amendments of the U.S. Constitution. Could they have adhered to the ridiculous notion that the clause in players' contracts allowing players to be renewed for the following season meant they could be renewed and held in perpetuity? Not likely. If the Continental League, moreover, signed multiple players from Mexico, Venezuela, Panama, Columbia, the Dominican Republic, Puerto Rico, or, when possible, Cuba, Japan, Korea, and Taiwan, could the National and American Leagues have avoided doing the same, especially if such players possessed superb talent? Not a chance, assuming they wished to remain competitive. The Continental League could have brought about the salutary internationalization of baseball generations before it finally occurred. In other words, the Continental League could have and would have induced a sea change in the way baseball thought about players.

Beyond the internationalization of baseball, an independent Continental League could have hastened the evolution of college baseball to the level it later achieved. Rickey talked of getting players from college as well as from the world. In the 1960s the Vietnam War had the perverse result of enhancing college baseball because it meant deferments from service for those players who went to college or stayed in college. To an aspiring Major Leaguer, a bonus from a Continental League team in the form of four years of tuition at a college of his choice would have been a huge benefit. To such a player who wanted to play professional baseball in the summer and go to college over the remainder of the year, it would have allowed the completion of a degree without the conflict of college classes and baseball. To accommodate such players, Minor Leagues operating from June through August could have been developed, just as the National and American Leagues began doing with their short-season leagues. For players who wished to play in college and not remain idle in the summer, the Continental League could have provided subsidies, no strings attached, to summer leagues for amateur players, including college players.

Territorial rights created a trickier issue. Except for New York the Continental League proposed no franchises in existing Major League cities. But obviously it would not have made financial sense to group new league clubs, or their Minor League affiliates, too close together, so some rule would have been necessary. Given the need to locate franchises in territory already occupied by Organized Baseball's Minor League clubs, the Continental League should have announced that it would recognize no unlimited territorial rights or pay indemnities. But it should have indicated that it would consult with the FTC to determine fair operating rights for each of its Major League clubs—a distance or radius originally proposed in Congress by antimonopoly advocates as thirty-five or forty miles. That radius might have been expanded based on population density, but not in contravention of the meaning of the Clayton Act. Whether that action would have led the National or the American League to adjust its thinking about territorial rights is an open question.

His many superlative qualities aside, Branch Rickey was not the person to lead the Continental League toward the reformation of baseball. He was unrivaled in baseball as an interlocutor, but he was burdened with serious shortcomings.

As president of the Continental League, Rickey manifested an interesting intellectual dichotomy. Throughout his long life, both inside and outside baseball, he had been an outspoken proponent of vigorous, aggressive free-market competition, and he railed against socialism in all its iterations. His contempt for labor organizers and the power of unions was as palpable as that of any other solid, conservative Republican. He did not deal with player representatives or have much sympathy for players' rights. He did not trust his fellow owners as far as he could throw them. He considered himself part of a cut-throat business, one in which he had managed, through sharp dealing, assessment of talent, and astute management of budgets, to excel better than almost anyone. He wanted baseball to continue on that path, or so everything in his life would suggest—a course he knew best. That was one part of his thinking.

The other part is more complicated. He saw the Continental League as a corporate entity, like U.S. Steel, in which a pool of scouts working for the company at large could identify workers (players) and then assign them to those parts of the corporation needing, or wanting, them most. Workers could be reserved in various units of the company, but only in limited numbers by each unit. Workers would be free to leave the company but while employed therein they would be required to abide by the rules on salary and benefits that the corporation established. Workers (players) could be traded or sold from one area to another. Historically this part of the paradigm allowed Rickey, a lawyer, to believe that he sold and traded contracts, not players, in all his player transactions—and thus that he never violated the Thirteenth and Fourteenth Amendments to the U.S. Constitution. He was simply moving talent around within the corporation, something evidence suggests he always believed, at least to some extent. Within the Continental League corporate unit, he would pool television revenue equally and give visiting ball clubs large portions of the home ball club's gate receipts. All Minor League ball clubs would answer to and be run by the larger corporate unit and not individual Continental League clubs. That is what the old baseball icon, the maven of free enterprise, had come to in 1959 and 1960. Did he harbor these same views about the baseball enterprise, or hold many of these opinions, over a much longer period? Probably so.

Beyond all that, he was old. He was infirm. He was too constrained by his customary way of doing things, by his corporatist thinking and personal history in baseball. He would draft players, hence limiting their choices and freedom of mobility. He would buy players. He would sell players for "money value." He would pay players poorly with salaries as low as he felt free to force upon them. He had no intention, though he made it part of his battle in 1959–60, to live in a baseball world without a reserve clause. He might limit the number of players any team or part of the corporation could control, as he sought to do in supporting the Kefauver legislation, but he would not give up the reserve clause entirely. Too much in baseball depended on the right to hold players for extended periods. Ford Frick said it best when he testified that a "reticulated" system had evolved, dependent on that one paragraph in players' contracts. Rickey would have insisted on territorial rights as well, modified perhaps, but certainly maintained. Despite his flowery, sometimes strident rhetoric of 1959–60, he was no modern-day Ban Johnson capable of making major changes in baseball through the vehicle of a new league—or, in any event, of the kind necessary in 1960 as opposed to 1901–3.

Coincidentally, such a person existed, and he had led the effort in Senator Kefauver's office to help the Continental League: Rand Dixon (Paul Randall Dixon), an inveterate opponent of monopoly, a stalwart proponent of free markets, markets unfettered by corporate domination. Dixon, a Vanderbilt undergraduate who went on to earn a law degree from the University of Florida, was a warm friend of the Continental League. As his appointment in 1961 as chairman of the Federal Trade Commission attests, his traits of mind and personality would have accorded well with the requirements of the new league. Moreover, no one in government understood monopoly behavior, the provisions of the Clayton Act, or the standard practices of baseball's moguls better than Rand Dixon.

The aftermath of the fight for the Continental League— and its demise on that hot Chicago day in early August—is too well known to give much attention here. Minneapolis-St. Paul got the Washington Senators, with an expansion team going to Washington. Los Angeles became the other American League expansion franchise in 1961. Houston and New York joined the National League in 1962.

Rickey flew back to New York and then to Pittsburgh and ultimately moved to St. Louis, where the Cardinals for a time employed his services. He did not like expansion in the way it was done. "You know, of course," he told Jack Kent Cooke, "that the internal expansion idea does not have my support as the best solution." He wrote to O'Malley on August 29: "It is my set opinion that internal expansion, so-called, is completely illogical." He warned the expansion teams that the players they received would be of marginal talent, in many cases over-the-hill veterans who would help their teams win few games. And the existing clubs would charge an arm and a leg for this "talent." New clubs should be prepared to lose over a hundred games a year for several years, and after the initial excitement of entrance into the exclusive club, fans would drift away. Most teams would lose money—in large amounts. The owners in this expansion scheme should go forward with their eyes wide open: the standing members of the exclusive club were not their friends but rather cut throat operators, competitors who would do them in at the drop of a hat. "I stated to our Continental group," he noted to friend Gordon Ritz on August 29, 1960, "that the first four clubs to be included in the Major Leagues would have my sympathy."[10]

Bill Shea was ecstatic knowing he would get a team in New York, thus fulfilling his original mission. But as everyone knows, the Metropolitans, or Mets, as they have been commonly known, became a Major League team in only a technical sense. They would be the essence of ineptitude, the laughingstock of the game, at least for several years. So would the other new teams (though the Los Angeles Angels managed to finish third in 1962). Some of the Continental League owners, most notably Jack Kent Cooke as a founding member of the third league, would be sorely disappointed at not being accepted into the elite club. As a group, however, the Continental Leaguers could eventually take comfort in the fact that all the cities in their incipient new league, except Buffalo, would gain Major League franchises, and all would at some point in the future achieve success.

Two final questions confront the historian. What would have happened to Major League player salaries had the Continental League become operative as an independent entity? What would have happened to the league itself? The answer to the first question is that in the short run salaries would have risen as bidding for players ensued. National and American League clubs would have increased salaries to retain their players, just as the Federal League led them to do in 1914–15. Bonuses for amateur players probably would have shot up dramatically as well. Moreover, no baseball league could have remained immune to the tumult of the 1960s and 1970s, and the Continental League, like the rest of baseball, would have experienced labor unrest. Such unrest surely would have contributed to pushing salaries higher. But a system, initiated in the Continental League, of no reserve clause and annual free agency would have kept salaries within limits—almost certainly much lower than they had become by the early twenty-first century.

The answer to the second question is that the Continental League, with its new ballparks, high-quality young players, and its aforementioned reforms, would have led Organized Baseball to some fundamental changes in the way it did business. Eventually, however, the Continental League would have moved, inevitably it would seem, into a structure not unlike that created in the merger of the AFL with the NFL. It would have been subsumed into a large corporate sports' structure with many of the attending qualities—some positive, many negative; some enhancing fan enthusiasm, some driving fans away; some contributing to the public interest, some not.

Organized Baseball and the Congress: A Review and Chronological Summary of the Past Ten Years

Prepared at the Request of Commissioner Ford C. Frick by Paul A. Porter, Counsel and Lobbyist for Organized Baseball, Feb. 25, 1961

VII. THE THIRD KEFAUVER HEARING

Early in 1960, the sports pages were filled with reports of the proposed formation of a third Major League, the Continental League. Promoters of the new league persuaded Senator Kefauver to include provision in his 1960 "Sports Bill" designed to assist in the formation and development of the new league.

On May 5, 1960, Senator Kefauver accordingly introduced S. 3483 (86th Cong., 2d Sess.). This legislation was divided into two sections. The first section provided basically the same antitrust exemptions for football, basketball and hockey as were contained in Senator Kefauver's 1959 bill, S. 2545, which had excluded Baseball from its scope. The second part of the bill was directed at Baseball alone, and proposed the following:

1. Application of the Sherman, Clayton and Federal Trade Commission Acts to Baseball, except as the bill (S. 3483) otherwise provided.

2. Antitrust exemption for contracts, rules, etc., relating to:

(a) equalization of playing strength;

(b) acquisition by a Major League club of absolute control over 40 players (plus 60 other players in their first 4 years of organized baseball), thus subjecting all other players to unrestricted draft;

(c) territorial rights; and

(d) the preservation of public confidence in the honesty of sports contests.

3. Condemnation, as an antitrust violation, of any contract, rule, etc., preventing, hindering, obstructing or adversely affecting the formation and operation of a new major league.

4. A 75-mile limitation of Baseball's regulation of television and other broadcasting.

On May 19–20, 1960, hearings were held before the Kefauver Antitrust Subcommittee of the Senate Judiciary Committee pursuant to Senate Resolution 238 (approved on February 8, 1960). There were only five witnesses: Commissioner Frick and George Trautman appeared in behalf of Organized Baseball; Branch Rickey, William Shea, and former Senator Edwin Johnson appeared in behalf of the Continental League.[1]

The representatives of the Continental League appeared first. Despite the potentially broad repercussions of the bill upon Baseball in general, their testimony related for the most part to the specific potions of S. 3483 relating to the creation and operation of additional major leagues.

Commissioner Frick and Mr. Trautman joined in opposing S. 3483 as being detrimental to Baseball. Specifically, the limitations on player control were often described by Organized Baseball as portending the rules of the Minor Leagues. Commissioner Frick reiterated the position which

Organized Baseball had stated during the various congressional hearings in the preceding decade, i.e., its support of ". . . the enactment of a bill which would give clear-cut exemption from the antitrust laws those aspects of the baseball business and the other team sports which are peculiar to them as league team sports and in which self regulation is essential." (Transcript of Hearings, p. 103)

During the hearings, Commissioner Frick emphasized, among other points, the financial support given to the Minor League structure from Major League sources. He pointed out that, in the years 1957, 1958, and 1959, the Major Leagues paid to the Minor Leagues through working agreements, defrayal in farm club losses, and direct subsidies for special funds a total of $16,443,711. All of these figures were exclusive of bonuses paid as an inducement for free agents to sign baseball contracts. Commissioner Frick emphasized particularly the fact that any efforts to legislate "player control" would remove the incentive for the substantial amount of financial assistance provided for the Minor Leagues. At the least, he said this would accentuate their difficulties and it could conceivably force their ultimate liquidation. Commissioner Frick, in support of his position, quoted Branch Rickey's statement before the same committee that ". . . there were no minor leagues if you withdraw ownership and working agreements."

On May 24, 1960, the matter was referred to the full Senate Judiciary Committee. Pursuant to a Committee vote on June 13, 1960, the bill was reported by the committee on June 20, 1960 without recommendation. (Sen. Report No. 1620, 86th Cong., 2d Sess.)

The Committee Report made several amendments to the bill. The most significant was the deletion of the provisions in S. 3483 stipulating that concerted action in opposition to the formation of a new major league would be in violation of the antitrust laws. This language was eliminated after the Department of Justice presented that it was unnecessary because the antitrust laws already prohibited such conduct.

Six statements of individual views were submitted together with the Report. Senators Kefauver and Todd urged passage of S. 3483 as amended. Senators Hart and Wiley, on the other hand, expressed in separate statements their opinions that the entire second part of the bill should be deleted and that Baseball should be included in the first section bestowing antitrust exemption upon football, basketball and hockey. Senators Dirksen and Hruska in a joint statement also favored equality in antitrust exemption for organized professional team sports, and added that S. 3483 should at least be amended with respect to its unrestricted draft provisions so as to protect the Minor Leagues. Finally, Senator Keating neither endorsed nor opposed the bill. In a separate statement he set forth as follows the care with which the Senate ought to consider S. 3483 (Report, p. 26):

". . . [W]e must exercise extreme caution with regard to any legislation which proposes to introduce the long arm of the Federal Government into the day-to-day operations of these sports. Self-regulation has generally produced honest and fair practices and any effort to upset these precedents and substitute Federal edict must be most carefully weighed."

Before the Senate began its debate on S. 3483, Organized Baseball prepared a statement of its position and circulated it to the members of the Senate. This document, entitled "Statement of Organized Baseball on S. 3483—Professional Sports Antitrust Act of 1960," was signed by Commissioner Frick, George Trautman (President of the National Association of Professional Baseball Leagues), Warren Giles (President of the National League of Professional Baseball

Clubs), and Joseph Cronin (President of the American League of Professional Baseball Clubs). Baseball's *Statement* made the following points:

1. Baseball's antitrust status should be equal to that of football, basketball, and hockey.

2. The unrestricted draft would wreck the Minor Leagues by removing all incentive for Major League support of Minor League clubs.

3. An unrestricted draft was not needed to enable a new Major League to recruit an ample supply of players.

4. Title II of S. 3483 would enable a new Major League, which had made no contribution to the procurement and development of Minor League players, to confiscate the very large investment of the present Major Leagues in Minor League player development and contracts.

5. Title II of S. 3483 was so ambiguous that it was bound to provoke damaging litigation.

Organized Baseball stated that S. 3483 would be acceptable if Title II were stricken and "baseball" were added to Title I's antitrust exemption for professional team sports. To effect this change, Organized Baseball supported the introduction of an appropriate amendment on the floor of the Senate. On June 28, 1960, the Senate debated S. 3483, as amended, recommitted to the Senate Judiciary Committee. This motion was agreed to by a 73–12 roll-call vote (Cong. Rec., 13687-88). The session of Congress ended with the bill still before the committee.

Reply to Statement of Organized Baseball on S. 3483 Professional Sports Antitrust Act of 1960

This statement of organized baseball sets out in its very first sentence as its leading objection to the bill that the proposed act **discriminates against baseball.**

First, it must be observed that the Commissioner of baseball, the presidents of the two major leagues and the president of the National Association (the minor leagues) have presumed to speak authoritatively for organized baseball. When they use the word "discriminate," they must have in mind defining the word as meaning unfair treatment.

After 60 years of ruthless use of power and pelf they now allege discrimination.

In what respect? Let us examine the facts.

They claim that S. 3483 would impose **regulations for baseball which are not needed.**

The statement should have added **not wanted by the existing major league teams.**

Yet, the unrestricted draft does help the majors and is much needed by the wealthy and talented clubs. Equalization of play on the field is of substantial value to any league and vitally needed by the financially weak or artistically impotent clubs.

Mr. Frick has said on several occasions that he is completely favorable to the unrestricted draft and very recently told one of the undersigned that he would go "all the way with him" on the unrestricted draft. Now he and others, who very well know better, allege in writing that the unrestricted draft is discriminatory against the majors.

On the point that the bill **would almost inevitably destroy the minor leagues,** the majors would not lose by draft a single player now included in their over-all list of 3200, except as those players become universally draftable under the four-year rule. The bill so states. It is not likely, therefore, that the passage of this bill could bring any reduction in their minor league affiliation during that four-year period.

Moreover, after four years, there will be at least one additional major league to support additional minor leagues, and it is to be assumed that, even after the four-year period, each and every club in the American and National Leagues will still have vigorous incentive to acquire the 40 best players throughout the country.

Surely they will continue to subsidize minor leagues sufficiently to protect and guarantee their choice of all players to be selected for their 40-player rosters.

Every major league will provide such exposure conditions to all prospective players as to enable the club to see its prospects in action before the draft date.

The Senators must not be misled into thinking that the unrestricted draft applies only to a new major league. All clubs in the American and National Leagues would draft in accordance with their present rules. A new major league would follow its own procedure. In the event of a conflict, the drafted player would have the right of election to play for the team of his choice. If the present majors cooperate with a third major league, there would be no problem and both factions would enjoy equal rights in the draft procedure.

Yet, these gentlemen state that the bill, in this first draft will **abolish hundreds of player jobs.**

On the contrary, the new major league will immediately employ 320 players at major league salaries and with all rights and privileges now accorded to present major league players. In this current season the proposed third major is employing 120 players in a small minor league that was refused support by organized baseball. This third major league now contemplates the holding of so-called trial camps for free-agent players during the present season, if this bill is passed, trial camps in plan and volume unheard of in the past history of the game.

The majors may not like this competition, but thousands of boys will welcome it. The majors may claim that this opportunity discriminates against them, but how can it be discriminatory when they have every right and opportunity to do likewise?

It is unthinkable that the majors will retire from the player production field. It is hardly conceivable that baseball should have fewer minor leagues than we now have and particularly is this true if a new major league comes into the picture. Baseball has shrunk from 59 leagues to 22 in the past eleven years, but those 22 may be further reduced unless, indeed, there is immediate expansion of major league baseball.

These gentlemen further state that this bill will **confiscate the major league investment in player talent.**

This statement directly controverts the provisions of the bill S. 3483 and saves the investment in the 3200 players under control of the majors by specifically exempting every one of them from the draft, as explained above. If there is discrimination in the bill, it enters at this point against a third major, but more particularly against a great many of the 3200 players who are really deprived of the chance for advancement within the next four years, because they will be desirable as members of the new major league. Nevertheless, they venture to say that the bill discriminates against the major leagues.

When responsible and mature men of reputable intelligence will make so deliberately misrepresentative statements, it must surely be motivated by "on-the-ropes" distress.

They further state that the bill **provokes damaging litigation as to the meaning and legality of the bill.**

This veiled threat of litigation is not consistent with the oft-quoted statement of the Commissioner made on August 18, 1959, representing, as he did at the time, the organized baseball committee, as follows:

> Mr. Frick. The members of the committee will support a third major movement and will attempt to avoid interference.
>
> Mr. Rickey. Would you say that again?
>
> Mr. Frick. We will support a third movement. It is the consensus that we will stand by the Columbus Resolution and stand by the third league. We have agreed to that.

But now we have the obtrusion of litigation.

And this first paragraph of the statement of organized baseball addressed to the Senators closes with this sentence: **Baseball's long and honorable record of self-regulation does not justify such treatment.**

Under the circumstances, only a mind capable of unmitigated effrontery and poetic license could conjure such a self-serving conclusion.

Baseball is treated separately in Title II of S. 3483, and differently from the three other specified sports, mainly because of the minor league system and the thousands of controlled players. This condition does not exist in other sports.

After several years of hearings, sharp differences were apparent, not only in legal status; fundamental differences were disclosed in the operation of baseball games from those of football, basketball and hockey. The problems of minor league ownership, player-control through optional agreements, draft, etc., were not duplicated in the three other sports.

Baseball in an inferior position is the charge in the final paragraph on page one with a dig at the Supreme Court.

The United States Supreme Court in both the International Boxing Club and Radovich cases, explained that its Toolson (baseball) decision was based upon *stare desisis* and was not authority for exempting any business merely because they were based on the performance of local exhibitions. The Court further concluded that the orderly way to eliminate error and discrimination, if any, was by legislation and not by Court decision. Congressional processes are more accommodative, affording a whole industry hearings and an opportunity to assist in the formulation of new legislation. The resultant product is, therefore, more likely to protect industry and public alike.

That is exactly what has happened in the formation of the present bill S. 3483.

If the Senators will read the first paragraph on page two of organized baseball's statement, they will perceive the assumption by organized baseball that the passage of this bill would permit such an interpretation **as all of the minor league players could be drafted by another major league each year.**

The bill does nothing of the sort. The assumption is not only misleading; it is untrue.

In the first place, "another major league" means the third major. Both the American and National Leagues are permitted by this bill to draft minor league players. And neither of those leagues, and certainly not "another," could draft "all the minor league players."

The four Continental League clubs now operating as Class AAA within organized baseball will have a very substantial number of players ready for advancement. The Western Carolina League, Class D, and the first minor league sponsored by the Continental as a source of player-supply, will, at considerable expense, provide many players to be placed on the Continental League rosters.

Even if the American and National Leagues do not draft any players (and they would have equal rotation rights with "another major league") the Continental 1) cannot draft any player at any time from the independently-owned minor league clubs and 2) if "another major league" were to complete its roster only with players drafted from the minors, the limit would be 320 of the more than 3000 now admittedly under major league control. And this figure would be substantially reduced by the number of players owned or controlled at the time by Continental League teams through independent development.

Why would organized baseball boldly mislead the United States Senate to believe that all minor league players could be drafted by "another major league" when the maximum available to that league is only 320 except as a means of stopping the proposed legislation?

The major leagues have suggested amending the present bill S. 3483 to give the draft rights only to major league teams that are included in the private organization now known as organized baseball. A new league, unless it became a member of this private club, which could happen only with the sanction and permission of the present 16 owners, would then be forever foreclosed from obtaining any players. The present bill does not permit a new major league to draft players from any independently-owned minor league clubs. It applies solely to players under direct or indirect control of major league clubs.

To date, for 60 years, there has been no inclination on the part of the major leagues to increase the number of club owners. Their violent opposition to the present bill is best evidenced at this time by the fact that these gentlemen representing organized baseball wish to validate the reserve clause, making it completely impossible for another major ever to get players and, at the same time and by the same bill, make it impossible for any group trying to form a third major league to be admitted to the organized baseball structure.

In this statement by organized baseball its "spokesmen" continue to ask for minor league control of the player's life for as many as seven years. This should be the greatest challenge to any legislator who wishes to protect the young ballplayer citizen who has major league ability in his first year of professional baseball. Yet, read this quote from their statement: **A major league club supports a minor league club in return for the right to train and watch players during their second, third, and fourth season in the minors for possible advancement to the major league club . . .**

After four years the player's contract is purchased by a major league club. Under the rules of the major leagues, this four-year player can now be optioned for three more years to a minor league club without the player's consent and regardless of the desire of fifteen other major league clubs to acquire his contract.

What in the name of human rights and common decency are the major leagues asking the Senators to do?

Are they insisting that the United States Senate shall preserve the right of a major club to "train and watch players" for seven years, players whose ability warrants and livelihood deserves advancement?

Whose equality under the law is more important? There isn't a boy in the minor leagues anywhere who is not now tethered by this enslavement!

Yet, listen to the appealing plea of organized baseball: to establish by Congressional enactment the monopolistic control of every young player in all this great free country, and for whose sake? For the sake of a corporate clique that cares not at all for individual rights or player advancement.

The unrestricted draft gives the player the chance to advance on the basis of his ability to serve.

But organized baseball closes that paragraph with these ominous words: **The unrestricted draft would abolish that right.**

What right? The right to "train and watch" a player for seven years!

Commissioner Frick signed that statement.

The 180,000,000 people in the United States, if given the chance, will grant priority of rights to the players.

On page 3 of their statement, the gentlemen of organized baseball say,

> **Mr. Rickey, President of the Continental League, has testified that there is ample player material and he has never asked for a meeting of a committee consisting of himself and the presidents of the American and National Leagues, appointed last August to deal with the Continental League's player problems.**

Why hasn't Mr. Rickey asked for the meeting referred to?

The suggestion of a meeting becomes a mockery when you are unexpectedly confronted day after day and week after week with apparently contrived delaying tactics that serve to defeat the completion of a league.

Why should the Continental League talk about buying baseballs and bats and hiring players when they have only five member-clubs? And when they are told by organized baseball that "you will never get a sixth club!"

What is the point of trying to have Senators defeat a Sports Bill because someone has not asked organized baseball to talk about players? Why, indeed, when organized baseball demands **one million dollars as tribute** for advancing a minor league city to major baseball status. The third major league's willingness to transfer the minor league franchise to a new and satisfactory area, thus insuring continuation of the minor league, has failed to lower these unreasonable demands for territory. At the very moment when the major leagues are saying, "You can't come into baseball," they wonder why the Continental League does not ask for a meeting to talk about players.

Organized baseball, on page 3 of its statement, asks, **What is an "unrestricted" draft? The bill does not say.**

The bill does not say what a "draft" is, either. The bill does not define the word "reservation" or "selection." In fact, there is no definition of the words "professional baseball player." The bill at no time in any of its previous forms or in its present form, explains specifically what is meant by "directly or indirectly owned or controlled" players. The bill does not define the term "voluntarily retired," "disqualified," or "ineligible." The bill does not define the "defense service list." It does not undertake to explain to the general public what a "non-playing manager" is or a "coach." To the completely uninitiated the words "world series" could be meaningless.

The bill uses the term "good faith," but it does not interpret the phrase as it may apply to the conduct of baseball clubs. This bill uses the term "unrestricted draft" more than once without quotation marks. It is assumed, quire properly we think, by the authors of this bill, that the general American public and the fans everywhere, the players and organized baseball itself, surely know what is meant by the unrestricted draft, just as they know what is meant by all of the other terms above referred to.

There has been a restricted draft in organized baseball for almost 40 years. Great dynasties in baseball, entirely legal and existing without objection under the rules, but with great unfairness to players, were built upon the restricted draft.

The "draft" means, in the parlance of baseball, and to the millions of baseball fans throughout the country, that a player's contract in the minor leagues can be selected arbitrarily by a club in a higher classification at a price previously agreed upon.

Many years ago three of four leagues in this country operated independently of organized baseball and were, therefore, not subject to draft. In order to have these leagues come under the canopy of organized baseball, a compromise was effected by which the major leagues were permitted to select or "draft" only one player from AA or A classifications, the two highest. All other players on AA and A clubs at that time, and for many years thereafter—and even now!—regardless of their ability or the major league demand for their services, could and can be retained by the minor league clubs through this one-player per team limitation of the draft.

That compromise has been called for these past approximately 40 years, a "restricted draft." The unrestricted draft simply means, as the questioners well know, the right to draft all players, with defined limitation. For example, the unrestricted draft now in the bill "shall not apply to any player directly or indirectly owned or controlled by any major league baseball club at the time of the passage of this Act until such player has completed four years in organized baseball.

These are not terms defined in the bill, obviously because it was deemed unnecessary by the Subcommittee and its counsel who have doubtless carefully analyzed and determined that the definitions originally outlined in the Sports Bill were unnecessary and that such definitions were readily obtainable through usage and practice.

It could be said in the connection that organized baseball is not overly concerned with the definition of "unrestricted draft." Some powerful clubs are concerned that its authorization might deprive them of a player made eligible for the draft by a second division team even though they have first selected the 40 best players out of their own extended organization. Such clubs wish to keep, perhaps, a number of players for the seven years within their control before needful clubs can get the services of a player regardless also of the rights of the player to advance, as stated heretofore.

The organized baseball statement undertakes to scatter further confusion by questioning the meaning of the words "owned," or "controlled." These words are understood and there is no hidden definition. Organized baseball knows very well that if a working agreement is in effect between a major league club and a minor league club, then all the players on the minor league club are under the control of the major league club.

No labored definition is necessary in these matters. The facts are in evidence and will always speak for themselves. It is difficult for a good many baseball people to question why this bill is opposed so desperately by these gentlemen who are undertaking to represent the ownership of the teams. Organized baseball very definitely will reap great benefits from this bill in five directions, resulting from the unrestricted draft:

1) The players can advance on the basis of merit.

2) It tends to remove the irrational bonus, thus saving millions of dollars for the majors.

3) It tends to equalize the distribution of player talent by minimizing the power of money in determining the disparity in club standings.

4) It increases minor league ownership of player contracts and offers increased incentive to scout locally and produce prospective players.

5) It helps to extend the game nationally and thus meet the needs and recreational opportunities of all our people.

If this bill is passed, surely within the next five years the gentlemen who wrote this statement for organized baseball will regret their effort to defeat this bill. They will be gratified to realize the security of the game as our great national sport. They will be happy with the vastly increased profits coming from a world series among three champion major league clubs instead of two.

The third paragraph on page four of the statement of organized baseball asks the question: **Can a player in organized baseball be compelled by statute to play for an independent "major league club . . ."**

The answer is "not if organized baseball can help it." The whole question is based upon the assumption that the "major league club" to which they refer is a club not under the structure of organized baseball. Is it the purpose of organized baseball to force a third major league to operate independently?

We now know, as everyone does, that the major leagues do not want a third major to exist as a partner within its organization. It is almost apparent that they do not believe a third major can, under the circumstances, operate independently of themselves. That could be true, most regretfully, fateful as it might be for the future of the game. It would seem that baseball is extending continuous challenges for a third major league to move without them. If the major leagues continue to make it impossible for a third major league to be admitted into organized baseball, then the only hope for the professional game in this country is for this or a succeeding generation to accept the challenge.

In order to influence the meditations of the Senate, the statement by organized baseball says that an independent "major league" would not be bound by any of the other rules of organized baseball, including the high school rules and those of the American Legion. The Senate has been advised by the President of the Continental League as follows:

> The Continental League is utterly opposed to the employment of high school players or American Legion players and goes further than that. The Continental League will oppose the signing of college players if the major leagues will agree to it. Neither I nor anyone else connected with the Continental League has ever said that the league intended to take American Legion or high school players. We are constitutionally opposed to it.

Nevertheless, they continue to bring that subject before the Senate.

Organized baseball continues in this paragraph to say that they "have built up over a 40-year period in cooperation with high school athletic associations . . . these rules." It has been only a comparatively few years ago that the high school rule was adopted, and was accomplished in spite of continued opposition by organized baseball for many, many years.

The colleges of this country have been striving assiduously for years to keep organized baseball from taking their players. The Continental League is unanimously opposed to this raiding process and, as indicated in the telegram above, will do all it can to bring about a long-needed change of the baseball rules in this respect.

Of course, any league not subject to the rules and regulations of organized baseball can adopt its own rules and regulations and could sign players from all sources, including the major leagues, and could have no player limits, and no salary limits.

Paragraph three on page four is an inquiry obviously made to raise the eyebrows of suspicion when it asks the question: **Can a player . . . be compelled . . . to play for an independent "major league club" . . . which calls itself major league, but may be organized by persons who are morally reprehensible or financially irresponsible?**

We must assume that the question is a thinly-veiled derogation, and as such, it is necessary to refer to the moral status and financial responsibility of the present members of the Continental League. Any degree of disparagement is resented deeply by those who have had something to do with bringing together owners of the Continental League franchises.

Surely it is not organized baseball's purpose to try to convey to the United States Senate that the organizers of the league would seek or that the public would accept, any new league that was lacking in either moral rectitude or financial competence. It may be noted that all Continental League owners are residents of their franchise-arenas.

For instance, the New York ownership offers Dwight F. Davis, Jr., and G. Herbert Walker, whose fathers donated two of the sport world's most famous trophies, the Davis Cup in tennis and the Walker Cup in golf. Another New

York owner is Mrs. Joan Whitney Payson, sister of the United States Ambassador to the Court of St. James.

The effort to expand major league baseball to Houston is headed by Craig F. Cullinan, Jr., son and grandson of Texas oil-industry pioneers. In Dallas-Fort Worth the Continental League is represented by two more Texans who symbolize moral financial integrity, Amon Carter, Jr., of publishing, aircraft and philanthropy; and J. W. Bateson, a leader in construction, banking and civic affairs.

Organized baseball knows, through our detailed reports of August 18, 1959, that Mr. Wheelock Whitney, finance and transportation executive, heads the Minneapolis-St. Paul ownership in association with members of prominent families in that area, the Daytons, the Swans, the Ritzes, father and son, and others, many of whom are substantial bondholders who helped finance the beautiful and modern Metropolitan Stadium in the sole expectation of getting major league baseball. Today that expectation can be realized only through the operation of the Continental League.

President of the Buffalo franchise is Mr. John Stiglmeier, a baseball operator known in organized baseball particularly for his success over the years. Chairman of his Board is Mr. Reginald B. Taylor, long prominent in finance and philanthropy.

The development of the vast southeastern territory, with Atlanta as hub of major league baseball in the future, has been spearheaded almost single-handedly by Mr. F. Eaton Chalkley whose moral and financial responsibility has inspired two counties to vie for the privilege of building a great new sports stadium for his use.

Mr. Robert Howsam, able owner of the Denver Stadium and its occupants, the Bears in the American Association, and radio stations, is a son-in-law of former United

States Senator and Governor of Colorado, the Honorable Edwin C. Johnson.

The Toronto franchise in the Continental League is owned entirely by Mr. Jack Kent Cooke, whose devotion to and enthusiasm for baseball makes him a veritable pillar of the game. To raise the question of integrity, merely by innuendo, with Mr. Cooke in the League, is a reflection on the questioner.

The Senators, we are confident, will quickly recognize the spirit with which the question of moral reprehension and financial irresponsibility was raised on page three.

We hope and trust that the United States Senators, who are the only tribunal for their support, will, through this bill S. 3483, provide 180,000,000 Americans with the growth and expansion of our national game and bestow a new freedom of opportunity for baseball players.

Respectfully submitted,
Edwin C. Johnson
Branch Rickey
William A. Shea
JUNE 21, 1960

NOTES

1. An Odyssey through Life and Baseball

1. Lowenfish, *Branch Rickey*, 533–79; Shapiro, *Bottom of the Ninth*. My own beginning work on the Continental League predated these two books. See Buhite, "Continental League."

2. The Continental League Conceived

1. See Murdock, *Ban Johnson*, for a summary of Johnson's life and his founding of the American League. See also Rader, *Baseball*, 86–91. Alexander, *Our Game*, 76–86, also provides an excellent account of Johnson's career, his establishment of the new league, and the National Agreement of 1903.

2. Shapiro, *Bottom of the Ninth*, 23–26.

3. Shapiro, *Bottom of the Ninth*, 26. Individual baseball records come from the following websites: http://Baseball-Reference.com and http://Minors@Baseball-Reference.com.

4. R. Terrell, "Third League Cities," 31; obituary for William Shea.

5. *Sporting News*, May 21, 1958, 1. See also Rickey's draft memorandum of February 8, 1959, box 37, folder 1, Branch Rickey Papers, Manuscripts Division, Library of Congress, Washington DC (hereafter cited as Rickey Papers).

6. This sketch of Rickey is based on Lee Lowenfish's outstanding biography. See the section on his experience in Pittsburgh, 505–32.

7. Shapiro, *Bottom of the Ninth*, 30, 20–21.

8. Branch Rickey, notes of July 27, 1959, box 37, folder 1, Rickey Papers; Lowenfish, *Branch Rickey*, 548–49.

9. Havill, *Last Mogul*, xv–xvii, 89, 99–100. See also Johnson and Wolff, *Encyclopedia of Minor League Baseball*, for the standings and attendance figures for the Toronto ball club in the 1950s.

10.This account of Kirksey's life is based on the biographical note in the introduction to the George Kirksey Collection, 1910–1971, University of Houston Libraries; Titchener, *George Kirksey Story*, 37, 49, 64, 75–79; and Shapiro, *Bottom of the Ninth*, 43–48.

11.Howsam, *My Life in Sports*, 5–7; Lowenfish, *Branch Rickey*, 550.

12. Weiner, *Stadium Games*, 42.

13. See Branch Rickey, memo of conversation with John Galbreath, July 27, 1959; notes by Rickey, July 17, 27, 1959, box 37, folder 1, Rickey Papers. For the naming of the new league, see comment by Ed Johnson, n.d., box 36, folder 4, Rickey Papers.

14. Lowenfish, *Branch Rickey*, 559. For information on Rickey's appointment see the announcement of August 18, 1959, box 37, folder 1, Rickey Papers.

15. Rickey memo, October 14, 1959, box 35, folder 12, Rickey Papers. Mann at first opposed the Continental League but changed his mind. Rickey to Mann, December 31, 1959; Rickey to F. Eaton Chalkley, February 9, 1960, box 35, folder 12, Rickey Papers. For the record and attendance of the Atlanta ball club, see Lloyd and Wolff, *Encyclopedia of Minor League Baseball*, 297.

16. Minutes of a meeting of Continental League officials, March 8, 1960, box 39, folder 7, Rickey Papers.

17. Rickey memo of conversation with Mark Scott, October 17, 1959, box 38, folder 10; Rickey to O'Malley, January 15, 1960, box 38, folder 10, both in Rickey Papers.

18. Rickey memo, November 6, 1959, box 39, folder 12, Rickey Papers.

19. Rickey testimony to Kefauver Committee in Senate, July 31, 1959, box 38, folder 3, Rickey Papers; Shapiro, *Bottom of the Ninth*, 117–18.

20. Shapiro, *Bottom of the Ninth*, 97.

21. See Alexander, *Our Game*, 73–83, 102–7, 134–35 for an excellent summary of the American and Federal League challenges and their outcomes. See also Abrams, *Legal Bases*, 14–15, 45–69; and Levitt *Battle That Forged Baseball*.

22. Documentary record of meeting of Continental League officials with officials of National and American Leagues, August 28, 1959, box 36, folder 2, Rickey Papers.

23. See Major League Baseball rules for expansion, agreed upon by Major League owners, 1958, box 35, folder 16, Rickey Papers; Buhite, "Continental League," 433–34.

24. Buhite, "Continental League," 436–37; Shapiro, *Bottom of the Ninth*, 111–13.

3. The Horsehide Cartel Challenged

1. Memo of meeting of Continental League owners and Rickey with officials of Major League Baseball, 156 pp., August 18, 1959, box 36, folder 2, Rickey Papers.

2. Shapiro, *Bottom of the Ninth*, 137–38.

3. Rickey letter to Cronin, November 9, 1959, box 35, folder 10, Rickey Papers.

4. Frick telephone call to Rickey, November 9, 1959; Rickey note to Continental League owners, box 35, folder 10, Rickey Papers.

5. Shapiro, *Bottom of the Ninth*, 143–44.

6. Rickey telephone conversations with Cronin, November 10, 16, 1959, box 35, folder 10, Rickey Papers. See also Rickey to Cronin, November 23, 1959, box 35, folder 10, Rickey Papers.

7. Rickey-Cronin phone conversation, November 16, 1959, box 35, folder 10, Rickey Papers.

8. Rickey to Cronin, November 23, 1959, box 35, folder 10, Rickey Papers.

9. Draft by Rickey on "going independent," n.d., box 37, folder 3, Rickey Papers.

10. O'Malley to Rickey, November 30, 1959, box 40, folder 2; Rickey to O'Malley, December 6, 1959, box 40, folder 2, both in Rickey Papers.

11. *New York Times*, December 10, 1959; Lowenfish, *Branch Rickey*, 563.

12. Lowenfish and Lupien, *Imperfect Diamond*, 155–68; Goldstein, obituary for Danny Gardella.

13. Hylton, "Why Baseball's Anti-Trust Exemption Still Survives."

14. Hylton, "Why Baseball's Anti-Trust Exemption Still Survives"; Hylton, "Walter Kowalski."

15. *Organized Baseball and the Congress: A Review and Chron-ological Summary of the Past Ten Years*, pamphlet prepared at the request of Ford Frick by Paul A. Porter, counsel, February 25, 1961, Sen. Estes Kefauver Papers, Hoskins Library, University of Tennes-see, Knoxville. (Now housed in the Howard Baker Center for Pub-lic Policy.)

16. *Organized Baseball and the Congress.*

17. Rickey report, November 13, 1959, box 39, folder 2, Rickey Papers.

18. Standard Player's Contract, in the author's possession.

19. Rickey memo, December 8, 1959, box 35, folder 10, Rickey Papers.

20. Rickey memo of meeting with Rand Dixon, February 26, 1960, box 39, folder 13, Rickey Papers; Buhite, "Continental League," 440.

21. For the discussion of all these territorial issues, see Rickey report, June 6, 1960, box 35, folder 16; and Rickey to Ford Frick, June 1, 1960, box 39, folder 16, both in Rickey Papers. See also Grow, "Defining the 'Business of Baseball.'"

22. Rickey to Craig Cullinan, March 11, 1960, box 37, folder 6, Rickey Papers.

23. *Sporting News*, July 1, 1959, 10. The *Sporting News* editori-alized on June 20, 1960, that Rickey's pooling plan was "socialized baseball." See also Rickey memo, n.d., box 37, folder 3, Rickey Pa-pers, on the equity issue. Rickey thought a TV contract for the new league could bring in an aggregate $5 to $10 million. Rickey memo, n.d., box 39, folder 2, Rickey Papers.

24. Rickey to Lamar Hunt, July 9, 1959, box 36, folder 6, Rick-ey Papers.

25. Rickey memo of meeting with Ford Frick, February 2, 1960, box 35, folder 16, Rickey Papers.

26. *Organized Baseball and the Congress.*

27. Lowenfish, *Branch Rickey*, 568–70.

28. Rickey memo of meeting with Rand Dixon, February 26, 1960, box 39, folder 13, Rickey Papers.

29. Rickey memo of meeting with Ford Frick, October 12, 1959, box 39, folder 12, Rickey Papers.

30. For Kefauver's political concerns and his antimonopoly activities, particularly against the drug companies, see Gorman, *Kefauver*, 332–47. See also Buhite, "Continental League," 442.

31. For an excellent account of the political maneuvering, see Lowenfish, *Branch Rickey*, 570–72.

32. Memo by the Executive Committee of the Houston Sports Association, October 20, 1959, box 37, folder 5; Donald Labbruzzo to Rickey, n.d., box 35, folder 16, both in Rickey Papers.

33. Rickey to George Kirksey, January 14, 1960, box 37, folder 6, Rickey Papers.

4. The Western Carolina League

1. In 1963 with the addition of Rock Hill and Greenville, South Carolina, the league changed its name to the Western Carolinas League. After the 1963 season the venerable South Atlantic League folded. In 1980 the Western Carolinas League took the South Atlantic League (Sally League) name. The new-era South Atlantic League has prospered in no small measure because of Moss's leadership.

2. As its successor, the South Atlantic League continued all the records of the Western Carolina/Carolinas League. Hence, because I led the Rutherford County (Forest City) ball club in hitting, I am in the modern South Atlantic League record book.

3. Personal interviews with John Moss, December 3, 2004; October 13, 2005; January 6, 2006; October 19, 2006; March 8, 2007; June 28, 2007; November 8, 2007—all in Kings Mountain, North Carolina. Interestingly, Moss later used some of this same wording in assisting a sportswriter friend with his uncritical book on Moss. See B. Terrell, *John Henry Moss*, 4–9.

4. Moss to Dwight Davis, January 13, 1960; Davis to Moss, January 23, 1960, box 41, folder 1, Rickey Papers; Buhite, "Continental League," 450–51; Arthur Mann to Reginald Taylor, June 6, 1960, box 35, folder 16, Rickey Papers; Rickey report, n.d., box 39, folder 9, Rickey Papers.

5. Moss to Davis, January 13, 1960; Davis to Moss, January 23, 1960; Mann to Reginald Taylor, June 6, 1960; Rickey report; Buhite, "Continental League," 450–51.

6. Rickey memo of conversation with Ford Frick, March 28, 1960, box 39, folder 13, Rickey Papers; Arthur Mann to Hon. A.

Paul Kitchen, March 30, 1960; Rickey on WNEW, both in box 41, folder 4, Rickey Papers.

7. Bob Howsam to Arthur Mann, May 12, 1960, box 41, folder 4, Rickey Papers.

8. Lloyd and Wolff, *Encyclopedia of Minor League Baseball*, 245.

9. I enjoyed many friendly conversations with Early before and after games during the 1960 season. He lamented his earlier habitual drinking and its effect on his family and his career. The owner at Statesville differed mainly with Early's handling of his pitchers, insisting that he never relieved them soon enough. See *Statesville Record and Landmark*, July 20, 1960. After his release at Statesville, he signed as a player with Gastonia, where at age forty-three he played twelve games. Abstinence was important to Rickey. He wanted to use Billy Southworth, a former Major League outfielder and manager of the Cardinals, in the Continental League not only because no Major League manager was superior but also because "this chap [had] not had a drink in three years." Rickey, undated report, box 39, folder 7, Rickey Papers.

10. Minor League owners, usually interested in cutting costs, sometimes cheated players and managers with impunity. The Statesville owner did not adhere to the highest ethical standards in replacing Early. McCurdy fired Early on July 18 and replaced him first with one player, Gail Thomas, then with another, Paul Fouts. Fouts had been in Organized Baseball for thirteen years, but he was making only $300 per month as a player. McCurdy added $250 to Fouts's pay to both play and manage, even though the Continental League had provided the Statesville club $1,000 per month for the manager's salary. McCurdy pocketed the extra $750 per month. Fouts did not learn that he had been "shorted" until after the season ended. When Rickey learned of what had happened, he asked McCurdy to return the money to him (Rickey). Whether McCurdy ever did so is unclear. To Fouts, Rickey said, "Too bad, too late." Rickey expressed his annoyance with Early's dismissal in the same document. Branch Rickey to Fleet McCurdy, July 19, 1960, box 42, folder 1, Rickey Papers.

11. This information on salaries and working agreements is available but scattered in Rickey's reports and in his correspondence with

personnel in the Western Carolina League. See Box 41, Rickey Papers. Clubs did not make much money at the gate. Ticket prices in most cities were seventy-five cents for adults and thirty-five cents for children or students. Prices for the All-Star Games were ninety-nine cents for adults and thirty-five cents for students. Lexington, Salisbury, and Statesville drew the most fans: 41,000, 31,000, and 30,000 respectively. Others drew 14,000 to 16,000. Forest City drew 16,167. For Forest City this meant gate receipts of roughly $10,000 to $12,000 total for fifty home games. For Lexington it meant $28,000, give or take. How many admissions were adult and how many students makes exact calculation impossible. As of July 11, total receipts at Forest City were $5,219; at Statesville $10,201. Box 41, Rickey Papers.

12. Box 41, Rickey Papers.

13. The ball-in-the-shirt escapade was indelibly imprinted on my brain. I remember the play as if it occurred yesterday. Jack Falls, player and interim manager during Queen's suspension, told George Ferrell and me of Queen's tirade. In my meeting with him on October 13, 2005, Moss told me all the details of the crime against the umpires. Personal interview with Moss, October 13, 2005.

14. For reports on players and the unfolding of the season, see boxes 39 through 41, Rickey Papers. Included in these materials are regular accounts of events in the league, published in each of the cities' newspapers. See also the *Sporting News Guide* for the 1960 season, 367–73.

15. See *Organized Baseball and the Congress*, Senator Estes Kefauver Papers, Hoskins Library, University of Tennessee, Knoxville (hereafter cited as Kefauver Papers); and the following articles that appeared in the *Sporting News* during July 1960: "Buffalo C.L. Official"; Prell, "Majors to Increase"; Daniel, "Hot Reaction." Taylor Spink, editor of the *Sporting News*, was a staunch opponent of the Continental League throughout its existence. See, for instance, his editorial of May 25, 1960, "Continental Hasn't Justified Existence" and other articles such as Hurwitz, "No Monopoly in O.B."; Daniel, "Kefauver Bill Most Dangerous"; and Brady, "Frick Clears Sacks."

16. *Organized Baseball and the Congress*, Kefauver Papers. The Major Leagues had done nothing to foster health in the Minor Leagues, and for the next decade despite internal Major League expansion, the number of Minor Leagues did not increase.

17. The Western Carolina League was an outstanding organization, Rickey declared, whose players would command a market price far in excess of the $120,000 that the Continental League had invested in the league. See Rickey's report on players, n.d., box 39, folder 9; and box 41, folder 1, Rickey Papers. See also the *Salisbury Post*, July 28, 1960, for Rickey's comment, based on a game he viewed in Salisbury the previous night, that "he saw some players he wouldn't sell for $25,000 apiece."

18. Scouting report on Rutherford County Club, n.d., box 41, folder 5, Rickey Papers. After a game in Forest City against Shelby one night in midseason, a group of players and their wives or girlfriends were standing next to the concession stand having hot dogs and beer. George Wilson, the Shelby manager, called me aside and asked if I would like to go with him to play in Nicaragua that winter. He said he was going to take thirty players from the Western Carolina League to play in the Nicaraguan Winter League, that he was a good friend of the Nicaraguan president, Luis Somoza, and that it would be a great opportunity. He did not understand when I expressed only lukewarm interest. Though I did not tell him so, I had plans to finish college and begin graduate school as soon as possible. I also knew a little about the Somoza regime in Nicaragua. I never heard from him again on the matter, nor do I know if he actually took a contingent of players to that country. For the initiation of Wilson's plan, see Wilson to Dwight Davis, April 25, 1960, box 41, folder 1, Rickey Papers.

19. *Sporting News*, July 1, 1959, 10.

20. This information on the Western Carolina League, Western Carolinas League, and Sally League from 1961 to 1980 comes from John Moss in my interviews with him in Kings Mountain, North Carolina, on November 8, 2007; and from an unpublished manuscript prepared by Cecil Darby, a sportswriter and friend of Moss— the manuscript then in Moss's possession.

5. The Continental League Undercut

1. This account of the American Football League is based on Gruver, *American Football League*, 9–73, 155–246; and Jack Horrigan, *Other League*, 1–222.

2. An exasperated Rickey at one point in the fall of 1959 observed, "Most of the organized opposition comes from the New York Yankees." Branch Rickey, report, November 13, 1959, box 39, folder 2, Rickey Papers.

3. See Shapiro, *Bottom of the Ninth*, 169–71.

4. "Buffalo C.L. Official"; Prell, "Majors to Increase"; Daniel, "Hot Reaction"; Shapiro, *Bottom of the Ninth*, 207–12.

5. "Buffalo C.L. Official"; Prell, "Majors to Increase"; Daniel, "Hot Reaction"; Shapiro, *Bottom of the Ninth*, 207–12.

6. Lowenfish, *Branch Rickey*, 573–74.

7. Lowenfish, *Branch Rickey*, 573–74.

8. See Rickey memo of conversation with Frick, March 28, 1960, box 39, folder 13, Rickey Papers.

9. See Utley and Verner, *Independent Carolina Baseball League*, 44–232.

10. For these comments by Rickey, see Rickey to Jack Kent Cooke, August 29, 1960, box 39, folder 10; Rickey to O'Malley, August 29, 1960, box 39, folder 10; Rickey to Gordon H. Ritz, August 29, folder 10, all in Rickey Papers.

Appendix

1. The printed transcript of testimony and exhibits consists of 178 pages. *Organized Professional Team Sports—1960, Hearings before the Subcommittee on Antitrust Monopoly of the Committee on the Judiciary, United States Senate Eighty-Sixth Congress, Second Session, Pursuant to S. Res, 86th Congress, on S. 3483, May 19 and 20, 1960.*

BIBLIOGRAPHY

Archival Sources

Kefauver, Senator Estes. Papers. Hoskins Library. University of Tennessee, Knoxville. (Now housed in the Howard H. Baker Center for Public Policy.)

Kirksey, George. Collection, 1910–1971. M. D. Anderson Library. Department of Special Collections and Archives. University of Houston Libraries, Houston, Texas.

Rickey, Branch. Papers. Manuscripts Division. Library of Congress, Washington DC.

Published Sources

Abrams, Roger I. *Legal Bases: Baseball and the Law.* Philadelphia: Temple University Press, 1998.

Alexander, Charles. *Breaking the Slump.* New York: Columbia University Press, 2003.

———. *Our Game: An American Baseball History.* New York: Henry Holt, 1991.

"Baseball Coattails on Fire." *Sports Illustrated*, November 24, 1958, 30.

"Baseball: Who's Bluffing Whom?" *Newsweek*, August 1, 1960, 72.

"Big Hopes from Tiny Flicker." *Sporting News*, May 25, 1960, 1.

"Bison Eye '61 Continental Start, Buy Four from Phils." *Sporting News*, May 11, 1960, 29.

Brady, Dave. "Changes in Kefauver's Bill Jolt Continental's Chances." *Sporting News*, June 1, 1960, 13–14.

———. "C.L. Hopes Fade after Sport Bill's Failure in Senate." *Sporting News*, July 6, 1960, 8.

———. "C.L. Wins Two Points on Draft Provisions in Kefauver's Bill." *Sporting News*, June 15, 1960, 4.

———. "Frick Clears Sacks Testifying against Kefauver Sport Bill." *Sporting News*, May 25, 1960, 9.

———. "Long, Rocky Route Ahead for Kefauver Bill; Action Unlikely." *Sporting News*, June 22, 1960, 15.

———. "Rickey, Trautman, Frick Will Testify on Kefauver's Bill." *Sporting News*, May 18, 1960, 7.

Breslin, Jimmy. *Can't Anybody Here Play This Game?* New York: Viking Press, 1963.

"B.R., like Tom Jefferson, Prefers Dangerous Freedom." *Sporting News*, May 25, 1960.

"Bring Your Own Glove." *Sports Illustrated*, February 8, 1960, 26.

"Buffalo C.L. Official Sees Defeat of Bill as Body Blow." *Sporting News*, July 6, 1960, 8.

Buhite, Russell D. "The Continental League and Its Western Carolina League Affiliate: Branch Rickey's Second Finest Hour." *North Carolina Historical Review* (October 2004): 426–60.

Burk, Robert F. *Much More than a Game: Players, Owners, and American Baseball since 1921.* Chapel Hill: University of North Carolina Press, 2001.

Burnes, Bob. "Exit—Rickey, Smiling, and with No Tears." *Sporting News*, August 10, 1960, 4.

"Can Another Big League Pay Its Way?" *U.S. News and World Report*, September 7, 1959, 50–52.

Caro, Robert A. *The Power Broker: Robert Moses and the Fall of New York.* New York: Vintage, 1975.

"Certainty in New York." *Sports Illustrated*, February 29, 1960, 39.

Chalberg, Charles C. *Rickey and Robinson: The Preacher, the Player and America's Game.* Wheeling IL: Harlan Davidson, 2000.

"C.L. Official Claims A.A. Asked $5 Million for 5 Clubs." *Sporting News*, August 10, 1960, 4.

"Comeback at 77." *Time*, August 31, 1959, 39.

"Continental Divide." *Time*, August 15, 1960, 59.

"Continental Hasn't Justified Existence." *Sporting News*, May 25, 1960, 10.

Daniel, Dan. "Charges by Rickey Draw Quick Volly from Frick." *Sporting News*, June 22, 1960, 15.

———. "Frick Warns C.L. It Must Act in Hurry." *Sporting News*, July 6, 1960, 8.

———. "Hot Reaction to N.L. Bomb on Expansion." *Sporting News*, July 27, 1960, 2–3.

———. "'If Game Operates Illegally, Put Us in Jail,' Fumes Frick." *Sporting News*, May 11, 1960, 6.

———. "'Kefauver Bill Most Dangerous Yet Introduced,' Frick Warns." *Sporting News*, May 18, 1960, 7.

———. "N.Y. Gives C.L. Go-Ahead Signal: Board of Estimate Approves Construction of New Stadium." *Sporting News*, May 4, 1960, 1–2.

———. "Rickey Satisfied by Revised Bill—O.B. Maps Fight." *Sporting News*, June 15, 1960, 4.

———. "Shea Insists That Majors Carry Out Expansion Plan." *Sporting News*, August 17, 1960, 7.

———. "Third Loop Yelps over Report N.L. Wants New York." *Sporting News*, May 11, 1960, 6.

"Defeat by Innuendo." *Sports Illustrated*, May 9, 1960, 11.

"Deserving." *New Yorker* 35, no. 33 (October 3, 1959): 33–34.

Drebinger, John. "American League, in '61, to Add Minneapolis and Los Angeles." *New York Times*, October 27, 1960.

Effrat, Louis. "National League Admits New York, Houston for 1962." *New York Times*, October 18, 1960.

"Expanding Universe." *Sports Illustrated*, August 15, 1960, 8.

Foley, Red. "B.R. Threatens Drastic Steps to Get CL Players." *Sporting News*, April 27, 1960, 14.

———. "Rickey, Ex-Senator Johnson and Shea to Attend Hearing." *Sporting News*, May 18, 1960, 7.

———. "Shea Sounds Warning to Gotham: Claims N.L. Won't Return to City without New Stadium." *Sporting News*, September 7, 1960, 4.

———. "Unrestricted-Draft Clause Seen by Shea as Aid to C.L." *Sporting News*, June 1, 1960, 13.

Fontenay, Charles. *Estes Kefauver: A Biography*. Knoxville: University of Tennessee Press, 1980.

Frank, Stanley. "Boss of the Yankees." *Saturday Evening Post*, April 16, 1960, 31.

Frick, Ford C. *Games, Asterisks, and People: Memoirs of a Lucky Fan*. New York: Crown, 1973.

Goldstein, Richard. Obituary for Danny Gardella. *New York Times*, March 13, 2005.

Gorman, Joseph Bruce. *Kefauver: A Political Biography*. New York: Oxford University Press, 1971.

Gough, David. *Burt Shotton, Dodgers Manager: A Baseball Biography*. Jeffersonville NC: McFarland, 1994.

Grow, Nathaniel. "Defining the 'Business of Baseball': A Proposed Framework for Determining the Scope of Professional Baseball's Anti-trust Exemption." UC *Davis Law Review* 44 (December 2010): 557–623.

Gruver, Edward. *The American Football League: A Year-by-Year History, 1960–1969*. Jefferson NC: McFarland, 1997.

Havill, Adrian. *The Last Mogul: The Unauthorized Biography of Jack Kent Cooke*. New York: St. Martin's, 1992.

Helyar, John. *Lords of the Realm: The Real History of Baseball*. New York: Villard Books, 1994.

"Hold Your Fire." *Sports Illustrated*, July 13, 1959, 25–26.

Holtzman, Jerry. "Big Timers Clearing Decks for Expansion: C.L. Foldup Paves Way for 10-Club Loops in '61 or '62; Perini's Talk Big Factor in Peace Treaty." *Sporting News*, August 10, 1960, 3–4.

———. "Owners Meet, Back Frick in Fighting Kefauver Bill." *Sporting News*, May 25, 1960, 9.

Horrigan, Jack. *The Other League: The Fabulous History of the American Football League*. Chicago: Follett, 1970.

"Horton I.L. Executive Veep to Deal with Continentals." *Sporting News*, July 6, 1960, 29.

Howsam, Robert Lee. *My Life in Sports*. Privately printed, 1999.

Hunter, Bob. "Frick, Giles Roll Up Sleeves, Bark Back at Shea Ultimatum." *Sporting News*, April 27, 1960, 14.

Hurwitz, Hy. "No Monopoly in O.B., Cronin Says: 'First-Year Draft Helps Weaker Clubs,' A.L. Chief Asserts." *Sporting News*, May 18, 1960, 7.

Hylton, Gordon J. "Walter Kowalski: A Forgotten Man in the Legal History of Sport." Marquette University website. http://law.marquette.edu.

———. "Why Baseball's Anti-trust Exemption Still Survives." *Marquette Sports Law Review* (Spring 1999): 1–12.

"Int Club Blasts Continental Group as 'Bush and Insincere.'" *Sporting News*, June 15, 1960, 4.

"Int Nixes C.L.'s 120-Grand Offer for Buffalo, Toronto." *Sporting News*, May 25, 1960, 14.

"It Was Bound to Come." *Sports Illustrated*, August 10, 1959, 37.

Johnson, Lloyd, and Miles Wolff, eds. *The Encyclopedia of Minor League Baseball*. Durham NC: Baseball America.

"Kefauver Bill Could Wreck Game." *Sporting News*, May 18, 1960, 10.

"Kefauver Hearings Hold Up C.L. Talks on Polo Grounds." *Sporting News*, May 25, 1960, 9.

Kiner, Ralph, with Joe Gergen. *Kiner's Korner: At Bat and on the Air*. New York: Arbor House, 1987.

Klatell, Davis A., and Norman Marcus. *Sports for Sale: Television, Money, and the Fans*. New York: Oxford University Press, 1988.

Koelling, Les. "A.A. Says 'Nix' to Continental's Indemnity Offer." *Sporting News*, August 3, 1960, 28.

Kritzer, Cy. "C.L Low on Cash—Backers Face Loss." *Sporting News*, August 17, 1960, 7–8.

———. "Skid at Gate Blamed on C.L., Expansion." *Sporting News*, August 24, 1960, 33.

"Ladies' Day Is Really Here." *Sports Illustrated*, June 29, 1959, 31.

Lardner, John. "Seventy-Seven Is as Seventy-Seven Does." *Newsweek*, August 31, 1959, 81.

———. "Stop, Thief!" *Newsweek*, December 1, 1958, 85.

———. "Strange Doings." *Newsweek*, August 10, 1959, 56.

———. "The Teamless Leader." *Newsweek*, October 5, 1959, 84.

Lawes, Rick. "William Shea Dies in New York." *USA Today Baseball Weekly*, October 11, 1991, 4.

Levitt, Daniel R. *The Battle That Forged Baseball: The Federal League Challenge and Its Legacy*. Lanham MD: Ivan Dee, 2012.

Lowe, Stephen R. *The Kid on the Sandlot: Congress and Professional Sports, 1910–1992*. Bowling Green OH: Bowling Green State University Popular Press, 1995.

Lowenfish, Lee. *Branch Rickey: Baseball's Ferocious Gentleman*. Lincoln: University of Nebraska Press, 2007.

Lowenfish, Lee, and Tony Lupien. *The Imperfect Diamond: The Story of Baseball's Reserve System and the Men Who Fought to Change It*. New York: Stein and Day, 1980.

"Marquez to Become Scout." *Sporting News*, June 1, 1960, 31.

Marshall, William. *Baseball's Pivotal Era, 1945–1951*. Lexington: University Press of Kentucky, 1999.

McElvaine, Robert S. *Mario Cuomo: A Biography*. New York: Charles Scribner, 1988.

Miller, James Edward. *The Baseball Business: Pursuing Pennants and Profits in Baltimore*. Chapel Hill: University of North Carolina Press, 1990.

"Minneapolis: Big League Town in Waiting." *Sport*, December 1959, 22–26.

"Mr. Rickey Farms New Soil." *Sports Illustrated*, March 28, 1960, 38.

Munzel, Edgar. "N.L. Expected to Nab Houston and New York." *Sporting News*, July 27, 1960, 1–3.

———. "Third League Notes." *Newsweek*, July 20, 1959, 88.

———. "Time for the Shotgun?" *Newsweek*, November 9, 1959, 88.

———. "Welcome to the Third League!" *Newsweek*, June 8, 1959, 97.

Murdock, Eugene C. *Ban Johnson: Czar of Baseball*. Westport CT: Greenwood, 1982.

Nealon, C., R. Nottebart, S. Siegel, and J. Tinsley. "The Campaign for Major League Baseball in Houston." *Houston Review* 7, no. 1 (1985): 19, 26–27.

"The New League: Worth a Continental." *Newsweek*, August 10, 1959, 54.

"New Major League—The Cost." *Newsweek*, November 24, 1958, 71.

"Notes on the Third League Theme." *Sports Illustrated*, June 1, 1959, 31.

Obituary for William Shea. *New York Times*, October 4, 1991, D16.

Okkonen, Marc. *The Federal League of 1914–1915: Baseball's Third Major League.* Garrett Park MD: Society for American Baseball Research, 1989.

Organized Professional Team Sports—1960, Hearings before the Subcommittee on Anti-Trust and Monopoly of the Committee on the Judiciary, United States Senate, Eighty-Sixth Congress, 2nd session.

Paddock, Bill. "Frick Blasts Bill Kefauver Claims Would Help C.L." *Sporting News*, May 11, 1960, 6–7.

Patrick, Neale. "Continental Clubs Set Up Pacts with Class D League." *Sporting News*, May 11, 1960, 16.

———. "New W. Carolina League Attracts 5,826 in Debut." *Sporting News*, June 1, 1960, 38.

———. "W. Carolina Drops Continental Tie-Up: Wins O.B. Nod as Independent Loop." *Sporting News*, April 27, 1960, 39.

Pietrusza, David. "Big Apple Produced Big Sports Booster." *USA Today Baseball Weekly*, April 15, 1992, 44.

———. "Continental Troops Took on the Majors." *USA Today Baseball Weekly*, April 15, 1992, 44.

———. *Judge and Jury: The Life and Times of Kenesaw Mountain Landis.* South Bend IN: Diamond Communications, 1998.

———. *Major Leagues: The Formation, Sometimes Absorption and Mostly Inevitable Demise of Eighteen Professional Baseball Organizations, 1871 to Present.* Jefferson NC: McFarland, 1991.

Polner, Murray. *Branch Rickey: A Biography.* New York: Atheneum, 1982.

Porter, Paul A. *Organized Baseball and the Congress: A Review and Chronological Summary of the Past Ten Years.* Pamphlet. February 25, 1961.

Prell, Ed. "Majors to Increase to Ten Each in '62: Delay Action until C.L. Is Counted Out?" *Sporting News*, July 20, 1960, 1–2.

"Progressive Step by Senior Circuit." *Sporting News*, July 27, 1960, 12.

"'Public, Players Would Lose under Kefauver Bill'—Giles." *Sporting News*, May 11, 1960, 12.

Quinn, Kevin G., and Paul B. Bursik. "Growing and Moving the Game: Effects of MLB Expansion and Team Relocation, 1950–2004." *Journal of Quantitative Analysis in Sports* 3, no. 2 (2007): 1–30.

Quirk, James, and Rodney D. Fort. *Pay Dirt: The Business of Professional Sports.* Princeton NJ: Princeton University Press, 1992.

Rader, Benjamin G. *Baseball: A History of America's Game.* 2nd ed. Urbana: University of Illinois Press, 2002.

——. *In Its Own Image: How Television Transformed Sports.* New York: Free Press, 1984.

"Rickey Would Welcome Leo as Skipper of Club in C.L." *Sporting News*, April 27, 1960, 14.

Rosenthal, Harold. "Crew Could Change C.L. Park into Grid Stadium in One Day." *Sporting News*, April 27, 1960, 14.

"Says Majors Will Take All C.L. Cities." *Sporting News*, August 10, 1960, 3.

Shapiro, Michael. *Bottom of the Ninth: Branch Rickey, Casey Stengel, and the Daring Scheme to Save Baseball from Itself.* New York: Henry Holt, 2009.

"Shea Says Outlaw C.L. Could Sign Many in Majors." *Sporting News*, June 1, 1960, 16.

Spink, J. G. Taylor. "Talent-Supply Plan for 3 Majors Proposed: Program Would Give Continental Chance to Land Players." *Sporting News*, June 1, 1960, 11–12.

Terrell, Bob. *John Henry Moss: Baseball's Miracle Man.* Fairview NC: Ridgetop Books, 2008.

Terrell, Roy. "Third League Cities Pin Hopes on This Man." *Sports Illustrated*, July 20, 1959, 30–32.

"A Third League and Its Chances." *Business Week*, July 25, 1959, 31–32.

"The Third League: When—If Ever?" *Newsweek*, May 16, 1960, 80.

"Third Major League? A Look at Minneapolis Shows the Problems." *Wall Street Journal*, August 18, 1959, 1–2.

Titchener, Campbell B. *The George Kirksey Story: Bringing Major League Baseball to Houston.* Austin TX: Eakin, 1989.

"Umps No Problem for B.R.; Thousands at Every Contest." *Sporting News*, May 4, 1960, 2.

Utley, R. G. (Hank), and Scott Verner. *The Independent Carolina Baseball League, 1936–1938: Baseball Outlaws*. Jefferson NC: McFarland, 1999.

Weiner, Jay. *Stadium Games: Fifty Years of Big League Greed and Bush League Boondoggles*. Minneapolis: University of Minnesota Press, 2000.

Wendel, Tim. *The New Face of Baseball: The One-Hundred-Year Rise and Triumph of Latinos in America's Favorite Sport*. New York: Rayo, 2003.

"Western Carolina Will Open 100-Game Schedule, May 13." *Sporting News*, May 4, 1960, 38.

"What's Really So Tough about the Third League?" *Sport*, November 1959, 92.

Young, Dick. "The Big League Map Five Years from Now." *Sport*, July 1964, 26–29.

———. "Is a Third Major League in the Cards?" *Sport*, March 1959, 28–33.

———. "Mahatma Marked Exit with Matchless Line." *Sporting News*, August 10, 1960, 10.

Zimbalist, Andrew. *Baseball and Billions: A Probing Look inside the Big Business of Our National Pastime*. New York: Basic Books, 1992.